The Nearest Relative Handbook

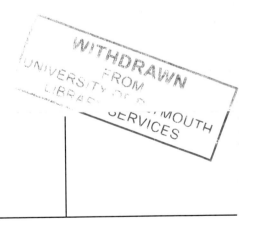
University of Plymouth
Charles Seale Hayne Library
Subject to status this item may be renewed
via your Voyager account

http://voyager.plymouth.ac.uk
Tel: (01752) 232323

of related interest

Community Care Practice and the Law
Third Edition
Michael Mandelstam
ISBN 978 1 84310 233 5

An A–Z of Community Care Law
Michael Mandelstam
ISBN 978 1 85302 560 0

Law, Rights and Disability
Jeremy Cooper
ISBN 978 1 85302 836 6

Advance Directives in Mental Health
Theory, Practice and Ethics
Jacqueline Atkinson
ISBN 978 1 84310 4834

Guide to Mental Health for Families and Carers of People with Intellectual Disabilities
Geraldine Holt, Anastasia Gratsa, Nick Bouras, Teresa Joyce, Mary Jane Spiller and Steve Hardy
ISBN 978 1 84310 277 9

Confidentiality and Mental Health
Edited by Christopher Cordess
ISBN 978 1 85302 860 1 pb
ISBN 978 1 85302 859 5 hb

Working Ethics
How to be Fair in a Culturally Complex World
Richard Rowson
ISBN 978 1 85302 750 5

Disabled Children and the Law
Research and Good Practice
Second Edition
Janet Read, Luke Clements and David Ruebain
ISBN 978 1 84310 280 9

The Nearest Relative Handbook

David Hewitt

Jessica Kingsley Publishers
London and Philadelphia

2013 → Plymouth

First published in 2007
by Jessica Kingsley Publishers
116 Pentonville Road
London N1 9JB, UK
and
400 Market Street, Suite 400
Philadelphia, PA 19106, USA

www.jkp.com

Library of Congress Cataloging in Publication Data

Hewitt, David, 1964-
  The nearest relative handbook / David Hewitt.
     p. cm.
  Includes bibliographical references and index.
  ISBN-13: 978-1-84310-522-0 (pbk. : alk. paper) 1. Conservatorships—Great Britain. 2. Capacity and disability—Great Britain. 3. Mental health laws—Great Britain. 4. Insanity—Jurisprudence—Great Britain. I. Title.
  KD737.H49 2007
  346.4101'8—dc22

                                                              2007015428

British Library Cataloguing in Publication Data
A CIP catalogue record for this book is available from the British Library

ISBN 978 1 84310 522 0

Printed and bound in Great Britain by
Athenaeum Press, Gateshead, Tyne and Wear

For my father, William Hewitt (1930–1981)

Acknowledgements

I would not have been able to write this book without the curiosity, promptings, assistance and support of a large number of people. I am grateful to them all, but should like to express my particular gratitude to Christopher Curran, Angela Downing and Mat Kinton, who generously agreed to read and comment upon this book while it was in draft. Any inaccuracies that remain are entirely mine. In addition, I am grateful to Joan Rapaport for allowing me to use her own indispensable work on the nearest relative. More generally, I should also like to thank my colleagues and friends for the help and opportunities they have been so willing to give me. They include Julie Austin, William Bingley, Tina Bond, Jeff Cohen, Stephen Evans, Malcolm Golightley, Catherine Grimshaw, Adam Hartrick, Chris Heginbotham, John Holmes, John Horne, Ann Meadowcroft, Mike Ogley, Egon Prtak, David Roberts, Georgina Rowley, Richard Stone, Gerard de Zeeuw, and particularly Bill Leason. My greatest debt of gratitude is owed to my mother, Anita Hewitt, and to my partner, Leigh. I know that to acknowledge my debt is certainly not to discharge it.

Contents

List of abbreviations used in this book

AMHP   Approved Mental Health Professional

ASW   Approved Social Worker

DMHB   Draft Mental Health Bill

DPA   Data Protection Act

ECHR   European Convention on Human Rights

ECtHR   European Court of Human Rights

HRA   Human Rights Act

IMCA   Independent Mental Capacity Advocate

LPA   Lasting Power of Attorney

MCA   Mental Capacity Act

MHA   Mental Health Act

MHB   Mental Health Bill

MHT   Mental Health Tribunal

MHRT   Mental Health Review Tribunal

RMO   Responsible Medical Officer

Introduction

Every so often, we are reminded that even now, more than a quarter of a century down the line, the Mental Health Act 1983 still has secrets to reveal. That is particularly so, perhaps, with the parts of the Act that deal with the nearest relative, and the reminders have come as often from Strasbourg as from the Strand.

The role of nearest relative, or something like it, has been with us for a long time. That we still don't know everything about it might have something to do with the legislation itself. One thing is clear, even without the intervention of the courts: while the means by which the role will devolve upon a nearest relative are unsophisticated, they are also strangely, perhaps unnecessarily, complex.

But that fact alone doesn't account for all the argument about the nearest relative. It seems there is a further complication; that we don't, in truth, know what the role is *for*. If, now, we like to see the nearest relative as a patient's representative, it seems that this hasn't always been the purpose of the role. In fact, it might not be the purpose of the role under the present, un-amended Act.

The Parliamentary debates surrounding the Mental Health Bill have revealed yet another complication: we still don't know whether the nearest relative is a good thing or a bad thing; a bulwark against the abuse of patients or a significant contributor towards it.[1]

Perhaps we shouldn't be surprised at the close scrutiny the nearest relative receives. Apart from that of patient, it is, after all, the only role in the whole mental health legal process that is not performed by a clinician, a lawyer, a social worker, a judge or a politician. Despite that, it carries some of the privileges the professionals have.

And yet, those privileges are enjoyed only at the discretion of the professionals. Maybe that explains why the nearest relative still exists, and why he or she will continue to do so; why even the most radical of the Government's reform

---

1   See, for example, Hansard 26 February 2007, col 1403 (Baroness Royall of Blaisdon).

proposals, which would have done away with the role, would simultaneously have replicated it.

I wrote this book because I felt there was still sufficient ignorance or confusion about the nearest relative to justify it. The position is unlikely to change if the Government makes the changes it has proposed. Those proposals are discussed here, and if they become law, they will be incorporated into any future edition of the book.

Two chapters are more abstract than the others. Chapter 1 looks at the changes the Government isn't now going to make, and suggests that what we'll get is less significant than what we might have had. Chapter 8 considers the place of the nearest relative once the Mental Capacity Act comes into force.

Those chapters apart, the aim of this book is a modest one: simply to set out the relevant law in a way that is clear and accessible. If I have achieved that aim, the book will be of interest – and use – to practitioners, patients and nearest relatives alike.

What is a nearest relative?

Once identified, a nearest relative will have significant powers. Those powers are contained in the Mental Health Act, but although the rules for identifying a nearest relative are firm, they are also complex. Furthermore, the Act could do more to prevent abuse.

Anyone who becomes subject to the Mental Health Act 1983 will have some of their principal rights taken away. In particular, they may be detained in hospital and forced to accept treatment for mental disorder, and they may have conditions imposed upon any subsequent discharge.

The Act attempts to balance this loss of rights by providing some important safeguards. The nearest relative is one of those safeguards. Most detained patients will have a nearest relative (and that will also be the case where someone is *about to be* detained).

The job of a nearest relative is to protect the patient by, it seems, acting in his or her interests. To this end, the nearest relative is given a number of powers. They include the power:

- to object to detention or, conversely, to apply for it
- to discharge a patient from detention or, less directly, to ask a Mental Health Review Tribunal to do so and
- to receive information about a patient's detention.

These powers should not be underestimated. Although few patients are detained by their nearest relative, many will owe their liberty to that person, either because he or she would not allow an application to be made, or because he or she understood his or her rights of discharge and was not afraid to exercise them.

The powers of the nearest relative are also subject to important limits, which, if he or she exceeds them, will lead to a person being removed as nearest relative. Crucially, however, it is only if he or she exceeds those limits that a nearest relative need fear removal.

The nearest relative is identified by a social worker, not chosen by a patient, and the rules that guide the process can be highly complex. This book explains those rules and gives examples of how they might be applied. It also discusses each of the powers of the nearest relative and the circumstances in which they might cease to apply.

The role of nearest relative is often performed by someone close to the patient – a spouse, for example, or a carer, a sibling or a child. This might be a logical, even a desirable state of affairs, but it can also create problems.

Although the nearest relative should act in the interests of a patient, it is not always clear where those interests lie. In any case, not every nearest relative respects the obligations of that office. Because, at the moment, they have no influence in the selection process, patients might be allocated a nearest relative who does not respect – or who may even have abused – them. Yet, by virtue of their appointment, a nearest relative will gain the right to make significant decisions, and to obtain extremely sensitive information, about the patient.

For this reason, the Mental Health Act 1983 attempts to limit the power of the nearest relative, but the restrictions it imposes are weaker than they might be, and in the last few years many people have called for patients to be given greater protection. This book explains such limits as there are on the nearest relative, and discusses how those limits might be strengthened.

A note on citations

In citing Acts of Parliament, I have followed usual practice, so that, for example: 14 Geo III, c 49 – which I have given as the citation for the Act for Regulating Private Madhouses of 1774,[2] denotes the forty-ninth statute passed in the fourteenth year of the reign of King George III.

I have also followed usual practice in referring to Her Majesty's judges: Judges of the High Court, who are more formally known as 'Mr (or Mrs) Justice Jackson' (for example) are referred to here as 'Jackson J' or 'HHJ [meaning His Honour Judge] Jackson'. The same applies to Lords Justices of Appeal, who sit in

---

2   See para. 1.2.

the Court of Appeal and are formally known as 'Lady (or Lord) Justice Hale' (for example): they are referred to here as 'Hale LJ'. Members of the Judicial Committee of the House of Lords are referred to here simply as 'Lord Mustill' (for example).

1

The Recent History
of the Nearest Relative

Although they are now well established, the provisions in the Mental Health Act 1983 concerning the nearest relative – and particularly those dealing with his or her selection – have become very controversial. This chapter asks why that is so, and it considers the Government's plans to reform the role of the nearest relative and examines how they have changed over recent years. First, however, a brief historical diversion might be in order.

Early history

1.1 In seventeenth- and eighteenth-century England, it was to families that the role of caring for the insane was primarily entrusted. But that caring role became harder in the nineteenth century, with the onward march of industrialisation and the attendant increase in urban living. Soon, the most significant role played by many families was to admit their relatives to the large new asylums. Significantly, even early admission documents tended to give equal space for the comments of doctors and relatives.[1]

1.2 The origins of the nearest relative might, perhaps, be found in the Act for Regulating Private Madhouses, which was introduced in 1774.[2] It required that private madhouses be licensed and introduced a process of certification for all but pauper lunatics.[3] Crucially, the Act also said that alongside the name of the advising physician or apothecary, the admission certificate should bear the name of the person committing the patient to confinement. That person was often a relative.

1.3 The Madhouses Act of 1828 went further, in requiring not only the provision of two medical certificates, but also that a relative of the patient positively *authorise*

1   Rapaport 2002, pp.75–77.
2   14 Geo III, c 49.
3   Porter 1987, p.152. See also Rapaport 2003.

his or her confinement. That relative, or a proxy, would have to visit the patient at least once every six months.[4]

1.4 In 1845 the role of relatives was developed further, when the Lunacy Act of that year gave them the power to apply to an external regulator, the Lunacy Commission.[5]

1.5 The next significant step was the Lunacy Act 1890, which gave powers to the husband or wife of a confined patient, or to his or her 'relative'. For the first time, the term 'relative' was defined. It would mean 'a lineal ancestor, or a lineal descendant not more remote than great-grandfather or great-grandmother'.[6] There was no hierarchy of such relatives, however, and no statutory way, therefore, of distinguishing between them. Once recognised, a relative would have the power to petition the justices, either for a patient's admission or for his or her discharge. For the first time, it would also be possible for a substitute to be appointed, who could petition on behalf of a spouse or relative who was incapable of doing so.

1.6 As far as discharge was concerned, the 1890 Act distinguished between a private patient and one maintained by organs of the state. The former could be discharged by the person who had petitioned for his or her detention, or, if that person was dead or otherwise incapable, by any spouse, or parent, or, by 'any one of the nearest kin of the patient'.[7] Discharge could, however, be barred by the relevant medical officer, who would have to certify that the patient was dangerous and unfit to be at large. In such circumstances, discharge would only be effective if it was ratified by two visitors of the institution in which the patient was confined, or by members of the Board of Control when it visited the institution.[8]

1.7 The Lunacy Act gave no such powers to the relative of a pauper patient, who could only be discharged by the authority that was liable to maintain him or her, or by any two members of the visiting committee of the relevant institution.[9] It would, however, be open to a relative of the patient (among others) to make application to the committee in that regard, but when doing so, he or she would have to give an undertaking that the patient, if released, would no longer be maintained at the public expense, and that he or she would be properly taken care of and prevented from doing injury to him- or herself or others.[10]

---

4   9 Geo IV, c 41.
5   8 and 9 Vic, c 100.
6   53 Vic, c 5.
7   Lunacy Act 1890, s 72.
8   *Ibid.*, s 74.
9   *Ibid.*, ss 73 and 74.
10   *Ibid.*, s 79.

1.8 These powers were supplemented by the Mental Treatment Act 1930, which gave a relative the power to object to the patient's confinement (unless he or she did so unreasonably or was unavailable).[11]

1.9 In the postwar period, the Percy Commission marked a watershed in the regulation of mental health care.[12] It accepted that relatives had a vital role to play, both in monitoring the need for a patient's continued detention, and in securing and providing aftercare. Largely for that reason, though it recognised the possibility that relatives might abuse patients, it suggested such events would be rare.

1.10 The Percy Commission did not distinguish between different degrees of relationship. It did, however, recommend that where there was disagreement about care, it was the views of the relative who was *nearest* to the patient that should prevail. This was the first sign of a distinction that would eventually resolve itself into section 26 of the Mental Health Act 1983 (MHA 1983). Where, however, the disagreement was between relatives of equal proximity to the patient, the Percy Commission said only that hospitals would have to use their own discretion in deciding which of them to prefer.

1.11 When Parliament decided to give effect to the recommendations of the Percy Commission, it showed itself to be rather more concerned about the possibility of abuse.[13] Indeed, Dr Edith Summerskill, who was at that time the shadow spokesman for health, voiced a concern that now seems somewhat prescient. Speaking in a debate on the Bill that would become the Mental Health Act 1959 (MHA 1959), she said:

> There is another point I want to make about the nearest relative. It is easy to dismiss this, but it is quite conceivable that the nearest relative is not necessarily the person most concerned to promote the welfare of the patient. [...] At the moment we are discussing imponderables, but I confess that I find it difficult to suggest an alternative. No doubt we are thinking of our relatives and that 'but by the grace of God there goes...' some of us. We should be quite content that our relatives should be there to look after our welfare, but can that be said about all people?[14]

1.12 When it finally emerged, MHA 1959:

- introduced a hierarchical list of relatives (which owed something to the Book of Common Prayer)[15]

11   20 and 21 Geo V, c 23.
12   *The Report of the Royal Commission of the Law Relating to Mental Illness and Mental Deficiency*, 1957, London, HMSO, Cmnd 169. See also Rapaport 2002, p.87.
13   Rapaport 2002, p.91.
14   Hansard, 598 736, quoted in Rapaport 2003, p.52.
15   Rapaport 2002, p.93.

- gave a nearest relative the power to detain a patient, or to object to his or her detention or seek his or her discharge

- permitted a nearest relative to delegate his or her powers

- included a mechanism by which a nearest relative might be displaced.[16]

1.13 The features of MHA 1959 were to be among the most significant ones of its successor.

The Mental Health Act 1983

1.14 The Mental Health Act 1983 (MHA 1983) contains the following provisions concerning the nearest relative:

- the definition of 'nearest relative' (and of 'relative')[17]

- the nearest relative of a child or young person in care[18]

- the nearest relative of a minor under guardianship[19]

- the nearest relative of a child that is a ward of court[20]

- the appointment by a court of an acting nearest relative[21] and

- the discharge and variation of orders appointing an acting nearest relative.[22]

Problems with the nearest relative

1.15 As we shall see, the nearest relative of a patient who is, or is to be, detained under MHA 1983 has a significant role to play. That role might include:

- applying for the patient's admission under section 2, 3 or 7 of MHA 1983[23]

- objecting to an application under section 3 or 7 of MHA 1983[24]

- receiving certain information about the patient's detention[25]

- discharging the patient from detention[26]

---

16   7 and 8 Eliz II, c 72.
17   MHA 1983, s 26. See: Chapter 2; Appendix 1.
18   MHA 1983, s 27. See: paras. **3.3–3.10**; Appendix 1.
19   MHA 1983, s 28. See: paras. **3.11–3.17**; Appendix 1.
20   MHA 1983, s 33. See Appendix 1.
21   MHA 1983, s 29. See: paras. **4.23–4.48**; Appendix 1.
22   MHA 1983, s 30. See: paras. **4.83–4.91**; Appendix 1.
23   MHA 1983, s 11(1). See paras. **5.30–5.43**.
24   MHA 1983, s 11(4). See paras. **5.69–5.73** and **5.74**.
25   MHA 1983, s 132. See paras. **5.77–5.102**.
26   MHA 1983, s 23(2). See paras. **7.2–7.33**.

- in certain circumstances, applying to a Mental Health Review Tribunal for the patient's discharge.[27]

1.16 The identity of the nearest relative is to be determined according to criteria contained in section 26 of MHA 1983.[28] Thus, a patient's spouse will normally take precedence over all other candidates.[29] However, the criteria are complex: for example, a spouse might sometimes be overreached by the patient's child, parent or sibling, and all of them might be overreached by someone with whom the patient has been residing.[30]

1.17 Crucially, the section 26 criteria are fixed and inflexible, and they do not afford a patient any role in the determining of his or her nearest relative. As a result, patients might find themselves with a nearest relative of whom they do not approve, or whom they certainly do not want.

1.18 The Mental Health Act Commission has drawn attention to the problems that can arise where, for example, the nearest relative has previously abused the patient;[31] and it has pointed out that the patient's right to be notified of a proposed MHA 1983, section 3 admission might enable the nearest relative 'to establish or re-establish contact with a patient in the most vulnerable of circumstances'.[32]

1.19 Because of the number and extent of the powers possessed by the nearest relative, and the concomitant possibilities of abuse, it was always likely that MHA 1983, section 26 would be the subject of legal challenge.[33] When that challenge finally came, it was grounded in the European Convention on Human Rights (ECHR).

1.20 Although the ECHR became part of the domestic law of England and Wales only in October 2000, when the Human Rights Act 1998 came into force, it has been available to residents of the United Kingdom for much longer. They have, for example, had a right to petition the European Court of Human Rights (ECtHR) in Strasbourg since 1966. It is Article 8 of the ECHR that has been particularly relevant to proceedings concerning the nearest relative provisions in MHA 1983. It states: 'Everyone has the right to respect for his private and family life, his home and his correspondence.'

1.21 The two most significant ECHR challenges to the nearest relative provisions in MHA 1983 came in the cases of:

---

27   MHA 1983, s 66(1)(g) and (h). See paras. **7.41** *et seq.*
28   See Chapter 2.
29   MHA 1983, s 26(1)(a).
30   MHA 1983, s 26(5)(b), (1)(b)-(c) and (7).
31   Mental Health Act Commission 1997, para. 10.10.3.
32   Mental Health Act Commission 1999, para. 4.46.
33   See, for example, Hewitt 1999.

- *JT v United Kingdom* (2002)[34] and
- *FC v United Kingdom* (1999).[35]

JT v United Kingdom

JT had been detained under section 3 of MHA 1983. She had a difficult relationship with her mother and wished her to be replaced as nearest relative by a social worker. JT claimed that because it did not make this possible, section 26 of MHA 1983 breached ECHR, Article 8. When the case reached the ECtHR, the UK government conceded that this was so. It agreed to pay JT damages of £500, together with her costs, and it promised to amend MHA 1983 (a) to permit a detained patient to apply to the court to replace a nearest relative to whom he or she reasonably objected; and (b) to prevent certain categories of person from acting as nearest relative. It was not evident from this case whether the Government was planning to make the necessary changes immediately or merely as part of its ongoing review of MHA 1983. However, an earlier case had given the game away.

FC v United Kingdom

The circumstances of this case were very similar to those of the *JT* case, and again, the Government conceded that section 26 of MHA 1983 breached Article 8 of the ECHR. As well as agreeing to pay the patient damages (this time of £2000), the Government promised to make a 'legislative change [which] would form part of a more general review of the mental health legislation in the United Kingdom'.

Honouring its promise

1.22 The Government has made several attempts to honour its promise to the ECtHR. They have all come as part of its somewhat protracted review of mental health law, which at one time contemplated the repeal of MHA 1983, but which now seems likely to end with the Act's merely being amended in several key respects.[36]

---

34   *JT v United Kingdom*, Application no 26494/95, Judgment of 30 March 2000; (2000) 1 FLR 909.
35   *FC v United Kingdom*, Application no 37344/97, Judgment of 7 September 1999.
36   See, for example: Hewitt, 2002a, p.194; 2002b, p.694; 2002c, p.886; 2003, p.661; 2004a, p.584; 2004b; 'Memorandum' [DMH 21] in Joint Committee on the Draft Mental Health Bill, *Draft Mental Health Bill*, Volume II, HL Paper 79–II, HC 95–II, Ev 279; 2005a, p.561; 2005b, p.966; 2006, p.613.

1.23 The Government's attempts have been contained in:

- a White Paper[37]
- a first Draft Mental Health Bill[38]
- a second Draft Mental Health Bill[39] and
- a substantive Mental Health Bill.[40]

The White Paper

1.24 In a White Paper published in December 2000, the Government announced that the nearest relative would be replaced by a 'nominated person', whose function would be to 'represent' a patient 'in discussions with their clinical team and in other matters relating to their case'.[41] The nominated person would also be a feature of the first and second Draft Mental Health Bills.

1.25 In the first instance, the nominated person would have been nominated by the social worker or 'other mental health professional' responsible for a patient who was to be made subject to compulsion.[42] This task would have involved rather more than simply selecting someone from a statutory list: there would have to be consultation with a patient's 'close relative or main carer' and the 'taking into account' of any view on the matter expressed by the patient him- or herself in a recent advance agreement.

1.26 There was nothing in the White Paper, however, that would have allowed a patient to choose his or her own nominated person, or even to block the appointment of someone he or she considered unsuitable. In fact, it was to the official performing the social work role that that privilege would have fallen.[43] Although the White Paper said that official should 'take into account' any views expressed by the patient,[44] it did not impose any obligation to adhere to those views. This state of affairs was little changed from MHA 1983 and would have been susceptible to challenge under the ECHR.

1.27 Furthermore, the White Paper stated that in deciding whom to nominate as nominated person, the social worker would 'be required to consult [the] patient's

---

37 See paras. **1.24–1.29**.
38 See paras. **1.30–1.52**.
39 See paras. **1.53–1.77**.
40 See paras. **1.91 and 1.92**.
41 Department of Health and Home Office, *Reforming the Mental Health Act*, December 2000, Cm 5016, para. 2.23. See Hewitt 2001, p.1202.
42 Department of Health and Home Office, *Reforming the Mental Health Act*, December 2000, Cm 5016, para. 5.6.
43 *Ibid.*, paras. 3.34 and 5.6.
44 *Ibid.*, para. 5.6.

close relative or main carer'.[45] Those terms lacked precision. How close is a *close relative*? How much care does one have to give to be a *main carer*? Can there be only one main carer? And those questions would merely have decided who should be consulted about the nominated person.

1.28 In many cases, the 'main carer' would also have been the most appropriate nominated person, and would therefore have had to be consulted about his or her own suitability for the role. Furthermore, the close relative or main carer might have produced a list of possible nominated persons, or suggested someone whom the patient hadn't mentioned. It wasn't clear how, in such circumstances, the social worker was to have chosen between the competing candidates. There might have been a statutory list, of course, but if so, how would that list have differed from MHA 1983, section 26, which Strasbourg had already ruled unlawful?

1.29 Finally, it seems that alongside its power to admit a patient to compulsion, any new mental health tribunal would have been able to appoint a nominated person where it was considered 'impractical or inappropriate for the person nominated to act on the patient's behalf'.[46] This power was clearly the Government's response to the cases of *JT* and *FC*, and it might have worked to the patient's advantage – for example by enabling the removal of someone imprudently nominated by the social worker. However, it might equally have had the effect of confounding the patient's own clearly expressed preference, and of perpetuating the breach of ECHR, Article 8 identified in the ECtHR. In any case, the old criticism, which the Government accepted in *JT* and *FC*, was that the will of the patient could be over-ridden by a single statutory player, the Approved Social Worker (ASW). Under the system proposed in the White Paper of 2000, no less than two such statutory players would have had that power.

The first Draft Mental Health Bill

1.30 The first Draft Mental Health Bill was published in June 2002.[47] It built on the proposals contained in the White Paper of 18 months before and had a number of significant things to say about the nominated person.

1.31 Had the first Draft Bill become law, compulsion would have been extended beyond hospital and into the community, and the ASW would have been replaced by an Approved Mental Health Professional (AMHP). While subject to compul-

---

45   *Ibid.*
46   *Ibid.*, para. 5.7.
47   Department of Health, *Draft Mental Health Bill*, June 2002, Cm 5538–I, cl 148–156 [DMHB 2002].

sion, a patient would have been entitled to a nominated person, who would have been appointed – though not necessarily *selected* – by the AMHP.[48]

SELECTION BY THE PATIENT

1.32 In the case of an adult patient, the AMHP would have had to appoint as nominated person anyone selected by the patient,[49] unless:

- the AMHP could not ascertain that person[50]
- the person selected by the patient was unwilling to act[51] or
- the person selected was 'disqualified'.[52]

1.33 In this context, a person would have been 'disqualified' from acting as the nominated person if:

- he or she was incapable of acting because of illness[53] or
- he or she was 'unsuitable' to act, having regard, in particular, to his or her relationship with the patient.[54]

1.34 This last provision might have had the effect of excluding as nominated person someone who had abused the patient, if that person had been chosen by the patient him- or herself. (There would have been an equivalent fetter upon the AMHP if he or she, and not the patient, selected the nominated person.[55])

1.35 No regulations were ever published, however, specifying the type of person a patient could *not* choose as his or her nominated person, and no guidance was ever given as to what might make his or her choice unsuitable. As a result, these proposals were viewed with some suspicion.

1.36 If the nominated person was unwilling to act or disqualified, the patient would have had the opportunity to select someone else, who was neither of those things.[56] But if the patient did not do so, or if he or she was incapable of doing so, it would have fallen to the AMHP to choose the nominated person.

48   See, for example, *ibid.*, cl 14(4)(a).
49   *Ibid.*, cl 148(1).
50   *Ibid.*, cl 148(3)(a).
51   *Ibid.*, cl 148(3)(b)(i).
52   *Ibid.*, cl 148(3)(b)(ii).
53   *Ibid.*, cl 148(4)(b).
54   *Ibid.*, cl 148(4)(c).
55   See para. **1.43**.
56   DMHB 2002, cl 148(3)(b).

APPOINTMENT BY AN APPROVED MENTAL HEALTH PROFESSIONAL

1.37 Before appointing a nominated person, an AMHP would have been required to consult any carer of the patient;[57] and before doing that, the AMHP would have had to speak to the patient, and to ascertain and have regard to his or her wishes and feelings in that regard.[58] The discretion would have been with the AMHP, however, and even if the patient had raised objections to his or her doing so, the AMHP might still have consulted the patient's carer.[59]

1.38 For the first time, the term 'carer' was defined. In this context, it would mean someone who 'provides a substantial amount of care to the patient on a regular basis', provided such care was not provided under contract or by a voluntary organisation.[60] It was never clear, however, how substantial or regular a patient's care would have to be in order for the person providing it to be his or her nearest relative.

1.39 Consultation – either with the carer or with the patient – would not have had to be carried out if it was inappropriate or impractical.[61]

1.40 When choosing a nominated person, the AMHP would have had to do so from the following statutory list:

- the patient's carer
- the patient's husband or wife, or partner
- the patient's parent or step-parent
- the patient's adult or stepchild
- a person of a description specified in regulations
- any other person the AMHP considered suitable to be nominated person.[62]

1.41 Anyone coming within a superior category on this list would have enjoyed precedence over anyone in an inferior category. This would have meant, for example, that a patient's carer would be the nominated person in preference to his or her spouse.

1.42 Given that he or she might have some expectation of being the nominated person, and that he or she would have to be consulted about any appointment in

---

57   *Ibid.*, cl 153(2)(a).
58   *Ibid.*, cl 153(3).
59   *Ibid.*, cl 153(4).
60   *Ibid.*, cl 177(1).
61   *Ibid.*, cl 153(1) and (3).
62   *Ibid.*, cl 148(6).

that regard, a patient's carer might, again, have found him- or herself commenting upon his or her own suitability for the role.

1.43 As with someone selected by the patient, a person could not have been appointed as nominated person by the AMHP if he or she was (a) unwilling to act as such, or (b) 'disqualified' from doing so.[63] (And 'disqualified' would have had the same meaning here – and been prey to the same uncertainty – as where the nominated person was appointed by the patient.[64])

1.44 Before appointing someone as nominated person, and providing such was not inappropriate or impractical, the AMHP would have had to ascertain the patient's wishes and feelings about that person's appointment.[65] But even if the patient was implacably opposed to the person nominated by the AMHP, that person might still have been appointed as nominated person.[66] The discretion would have been with the AMHP, not with the patient.

1.45 If an AMHP failed to appoint a nominated person 'within a reasonable time', a patient would have been able to apply to the new Mental Health Tribunal (MHT) for an order requiring him or her to do so.[67] (As we shall see, the MHT might also have performed a second, no less useful service.[68])

THE PATIENT'S VETO

1.46 Under the 2002 Draft Mental Health Bill, there would have been circumstances in which a patient could prevent his or her nominated person from assuming that role.

1.47 By giving the appropriate notice, a capable patient would have been able to prevent an AMHP or a local authority from:[69]

- consulting his or her nominated person[70]

- notifying or informing the nominated person of a particular matter[71]

- providing the nominated person with information about the matter[72]

- taking account of any representation made by the nominated person about the matter[73]

63   *Ibid.*, cl 152(4).
64   *Ibid.*, cl 152(4)(c). See para. **1.33** and **1.34**.
65   DMHB 2002, cl 152(8)
66   *Ibid.*, cl 152(9).
67   *Ibid.*, cl 156(1).
68   See paras. **1.49** and **1.50**.
69   DMHB 2002, cl 157(5).
70   *Ibid.*, cl 157(4)(a).
71   *Ibid.*, cl 157(4)(b).
72   *Ibid.*, cl 157(4)(c).
73   *Ibid.*, cl 157(4)(d).

- complying with a request made by the nominated person in relation to the matter.[74]

1.48 Furthermore, by giving the appropriate notice to an AMHP or a local authority,[75] a capable patient would have been able to prevent the nominated person from exercising any or all of his or her statutory functions.[76]

REVOCATION BY THE MHT

1.49 Under the 2002 Draft Mental Health Bill, a patient – or, in some cases, the AMHP – might have applied to the MHT to revoke the appointment of the nominated person.[77] The only ground for such an application would have been that the nominated person was, or was likely to become, 'disqualified'.[78] In other words:

- he or she fell within a description specified in regulations[79]

- he or she was incapable of acting as nominated person because of illness[80]

- he or she was 'unsuitable' to do so (having regard, in particular, to his or her relationship with the patient).[81]

1.50 Again, because no regulations were ever published, nor guidance ever given, it was not clear on what grounds a possible nominated person might be disqualified or deemed unsuitable.

COMMENT

1.51 The following points are perhaps worthy of note.

1. Even when he or she gained the right to appoint a patient's nominated person, the AMHP would still have been bound by a statutory list (albeit one with slightly more flexibility than section 26 had – and continues to have).

2. This list would have given precedence to a patient's carer. If that person was a relative of the patient, the list would correspond to the reality of section 26 of MHA 1983.[82] If, however, the carer was not a

---

74   *Ibid.*, cl 157(4)(e).
75   *Ibid.*, cl 157(6).
76   *Ibid.*, cl 157(7).
77   *Ibid.*, cl 156(2) and 154(1).
78   *Ibid.*, cl 156(3).
79   *Ibid.*, cl 148(4)(a).
80   *Ibid.*, cl 148(4)(b).
81   *Ibid.*, cl 148(4)(c).
82   See para. **2.11**.

relative of the patient, the list might have afforded him or her a precedence that he or she would not enjoy under the 1983 Act.

3. A cohabitee of the patient, whether heterosexual or homosexual, would have been entitled to be considered his or her nominated person, regardless of the length of their cohabitation.[83] This is because the definition of 'partner' in the 2002 Draft Mental Health Bill was broader than anything contained in MHA 1983 or read into it by the courts.[84]

4. The statutory list would have recognised step-relationships in a way not seen under MHA 1983.[85]

5. Where there were two or more people within a particular category, the AMHP would have been required to choose between them, not by reference to their ages, but according to which of them he or she considered 'best suited' to be the nominated person.[86]

6. By the use of regulations, it would have been possible to exclude as nominated person a broader range of people than those who were simply incapable of acting as such or unsuitable to act as such.

7. Although the right of veto would have been a significant one, it would only have been available to a patient who was capable of using it. An incapable patient would not have been able to prevent his or her nominated person acting, or being recognised, as such.

8. Even in the case of a capable patient, it is possible that if notice had been given preventing him or her from acting as such, the nominated person would have been among those whom regulations had deemed 'disqualified'. The relevant regulations were never published, but if this had been the case, a new nominated person would have had to be appointed, and that appointment would have been made by the AMHP, not by the patient.

1.52 There was a strong suspicion that the proposals in the 2002 Draft Mental Health Bill did not go far enough to satisfy the ECHR.[87] This was certainly the conclusion of the Parliamentary Joint Committee on Human Rights. It said:

> Under the terms of the Draft Bill the patient would have a veto on the nominated person exercising particular functions, while the patient was capable

83   DMHB 2002, cl 148(6)(b).
84   *Ibid.*, cl 158(4). See paras. **2.23–2.26** and **2.27–2.30**.
85   *Ibid.*, cl 148(6)(c) and (d). See para. **2.14**.
86   *Ibid.*, cl 152(6).
87   See Hewitt 2001, p.1193.

of making decisions. That would certainly be an improvement, in human rights terms, on the present position. But the patient would have no power to revoke the appointment of a nominated person or to insist on appointing someone of his or her choice. This would remain a potential interference with the patient's right to respect for private life under ECHR Article 8.1. The interference might be justifiable under Article 8.2 if it could be shown to be necessary in order to protect the rights and welfare of the patient or other people, and to be proportionate to that aim. We hope that the Government will put into the public domain the evidence and arguments needed to establish that the interference is justifiable in this way.[88]

The second Draft Mental Health Bill

1.53 The second Draft Mental Health Bill was published in September 2004.[89] It too had a number of things to say about the nominated person, and they weren't necessarily the things the first Draft Mental Health Bill had said.

1.54 Again, the second Draft Bill would have made it possible to exercise compulsion over a patient either in hospital or in the community, and it would have entitled him or her at least to select a nominated person. As before, however, the task of actually *appointing* the nominated person would have fallen to an AMHP.[90]

SELECTION BY THE PATIENT

1.55 The AMHP would have had to give a patient 'a reasonable opportunity' to select a nominated person for him or herself.[91] But this would not have happened if:

- the patient was not capable of making a selection and
- there was no reasonable prospect that he or she would become so capable within a reasonable time.[92]

1.56 In the case of an adult patient, the AMHP would have had to appoint as nominated person the person selected by the patient, provided that person was both (a) 'suitable' and (b) 'eligible'.[93]

1.57 **'Suitable'**: This term was not defined in the second Draft Mental Health Bill. Guidance on what it meant was to have been published in a new Code of Practice,

88   House of Lords and House of Commons, Joint Committee on Human Rights, *Draft Mental Health Bill*, HL Paper 181 HC 1294, 4 November 2002, para. 84.
89   Department of Health, *Draft Mental Health Bill*, September 2004, Cm 6305–I [DMHB 2004]; *Explanatory Notes*, June 2004, Cm 6305–II; *Improving Mental Health Law: Towards a new Mental Health Act*, September 2004.
90   See, for example, *DMHB* 2004, cl 19(5)(a).
91   *Ibid.*, cl 233(4).
92   *Ibid.*
93   *Ibid.*, cl 233(5).

but that never saw the light of day. It is clear, however, that the AMHP would have had a considerable discretion in this regard. The Draft Bill itself said a 'suitable' person would be one

> who *appears to the appointer* to be suitable to be the patient's nominated person having regard to all the circumstances, and in particular to that person's relationship to or connection with the patient.[94]

1.58 **'Eligible'**: The second Draft Bill said that a person would be eligible to be appointed nominated person if he or she was: (a) willing to act as such;[95] and (b) not 'disqualified'.[96] In this context, 'disqualified' would mean:

- a person of a description specified in regulations[97] or

- someone who appeared to the AMHP to be incapable of being a nominated person because of illness or mental disorder.[98]

1.59 No such regulations were ever made. The official explanation for this provision stated:

> Regulations will enable Ministers to disqualify certain categories of people from being nominated persons – e.g., it is likely that a convicted child abuser in the case of a child patient will be disqualified; a person under the age of 16 will also be disqualified.[99]

1.60 However, even if someone was 'eligible', the AMHP would not have needed to consider him or her for appointment as nominated person if he or she did not appear to be 'related to or connected with' the patient.[100]

1.61 In the absence of the promised regulations and guidance, the discretion to decide who might be suitable or eligible, and who might be insufficiently proximate, would have made it relatively easy for an AMHP to disregard the patient's choice of nominated person.

APPOINTMENT BY THE AMHP

1.62 There were three circumstances in which the nominated person would have been appointed by the AMHP, not selected by the patient:

- if the patient was not able to select a nominated person

---

94   *Ibid.*, cl 232(5) [emphasis added].
95   *Ibid.*, cl 232(2).
96   *Ibid.*, cl 232(2) and (3).
97   *Ibid.*, 232(4)(a).
98   *Ibid.*, 232(4)(b).
99   *Ibid.*, *Explanatory Notes*, n 414.
100   *Ibid.*, cl 232(6).

- if the person the patient selected as nominated person was not suitable[101]
- if that person was not eligible.[102]

1.63 These circumstances were the same as those which, in the first Draft Mental Health Bill, would also have led to the AMHP appointing the nominated person.[103]

1.64 The second Draft Bill differed from the first in not providing a hierarchy of candidates for the post of nominated person. For the first time, the person appointed by the AMHP would simply have been the *most* 'suitable' of all the 'eligible' ones,[104] and it would have been up to the AMHP to decide who that was. There was no indication in the second Draft Bill as to how the AMHP might make that decision.

1.65 If there was no one that was both suitable and eligible, the AMHP would have had to appoint as nominated person the appropriate local social services authority.[105] According to the second Draft Bill, this would be the one 'which appears to the [AMHP] to be most suitable to be the patient's nominated person'.[106] (Again, there was no hint as to how the AMHP might make this decision.)

CONSULTATION WITH THE PATIENT

1.66 Before appointing someone as nominated person, the AMHP would have had to consult the patient and ascertain his or her wishes and feelings about that person's appointment. This step would not have had to be taken, however, if it was inappropriate or impracticable.[107] The AMHP would have had to have regard to any wishes and feelings expressed by the patient on this issue, and he or she would not have been able to proceed to appoint the proposed nominated person if he or she considered that it was inappropriate to do so. In such circumstances, the person proposed as nominated person would in fact have had to be disregarded.[108]

CONSULTATION WITH OTHERS

1.67 Before appointing a nominated person, an AMHP would also have had to consult the patient's carer, or, if he or she had no carer, anyone else that knew the

---

101   See para. **1.57**.
102   *DMHB* 2004, cl 233(6)
103   See para. **1.32**.
104   *DMHB* 2004, cl 233(6)(a).
105   *Ibid.*, cl 233(6)(b).
106   *Ibid.*, cl 233(9).
107   *Ibid.*, cl 235(1).
108   *Ibid.*, cl 235(2).

patient, whom it was appropriate to consult.[109] This would be so where the patient had made the selection him- or herself, or where he or she was incapable of making a selection, or had selected someone who was unsuitable or ineligible to be the nominated person.

1.68 Before consulting someone other than the patient, however, the AMHP would have had to ascertain the patient's wishes and feelings about his or her doing so.[110] No such consultation would have been permitted if the AMHP considered it inappropriate, having regard to the patient's wishes and feelings, and to 'any other relevant circumstances'.[111] The force of this provision was diminished, however, by the fact that an AMHP would not have been required to ascertain a patient's wishes and feelings about the nominated person if it was inappropriate or impracticable to do so.[112]

THE PATIENT'S VETO

1.69 Under the 2004 Draft Mental Health Bill, as under its predecessor,[113] there would have been circumstances in which a patient could place significant restrictions upon his or her nominated person.

1.70 By giving the appropriate notice, a capable patient would have been able to prevent an AMHP or a local authority from:

- consulting the patient's nominated person about any matter
- notifying or informing the nominated person of any matter
- providing the nominated person with information in relation to any matter
- providing the nominated person with a document
- taking account of a representation made by the nominated person about any matter
- complying with a request made by the nominated person in relation to any matter.[114]

1.71 Furthermore, by notifying an AMHP or a local authority that he or she did not want him or her to do so, a capable patient would have been able to prevent the nominated person from performing any or all of his or her statutory functions.[115]

109   *Ibid.*, cl 236(1)-(3).
110   *Ibid.*, cl 236(4).
111   *Ibid.*, cl 236(5).
112   *Ibid.*, cl 236(4).
113   See paras. **1.46–1.48**.
114   *DMHB* 2004, cl 239(3) and (2).
115   *Ibid.*, cl 239(4) and (5).

REVOCATION

1.72 Where the nominated person appointed by the AMHP was someone selected by the patient, the AMHP would have had to revoke that appointment if:

- it appeared to him or her that the nominated person was or had become (a) disqualified or (b) unsuitable[116]

- the nominated person gave written notice that he or she was no longer prepared to act as such[117]

- the AMHP considered it appropriate to do so, having regard to the patient's ascertainable wishes and feelings.[118]

1.73 If the nominated person was not selected by the patient and, being unable to find someone who was both suitable and eligible, the AMHP had appointed a local social services authority to the role, he or she would have been required to revoke that appointment if:

(a) the patient, being capable, asked him or her to do so and

(b) it appeared to the AMHP that someone suitable and eligible could now be found.[119]

1.74 Having revoked the appointment of the nominated person, the AMHP would have had to appoint a fresh nominated person.[120]

THE MENTAL HEALTH TRIBUNAL

1.75 If, within a reasonable time, the AMHP had not appointed a nominated person, the patient would have been able to apply to a MHT for an order requiring him or her to do so.[121] (The patient would have had the same right under the first Draft Mental Health Bill.[122])

1.76 Where a nominated person had been appointed by an AMHP because the patient had not selected anyone as his or her nominated person, or had selected someone unsuitable or ineligible, the patient would have been able to apply to the MHT.[123] Upon any such application, the MHT would have been able either to

---

116   *Ibid.*, cl 241(1)(a) and (b) and cl 233(6)(b). See paras. **1.57** and **1.58**.
117   *Ibid.*, cl 241(1)(c).
118   *Ibid.*, cl 241(1)(d).
119   *Ibid.*, cl 241(2) and (4).
120   *Ibid.*, cl 242(5)(b).
121   *Ibid.*, cl 243(1).
122   See para. **1.45**.
123   *DMHB* 2004, cl 243(2).

confirm the appointment,[124] or to revoke it and require the AMHP to appoint someone else as nominated person.[125]

COMMENT

1.77 The following points are perhaps worthy of note:

1. It would probably have been easier to disregard the patient's choice of nominated person under the 2004 Draft Bill than under the 2002 Draft Bill. Though each would have ruled out a nominated person who was incapable of acting as such, or was excluded by regulations or unsuitable, the 2004 Draft Bill would have permitted the AMHP to ignore someone who did not appear to be related to or connected with the patient. No such power was contained in the 2002 Draft Bill.

2. For the first time, there was no statutory list in the 2004 Draft Bill to guide (or restrict) an AMHP in his or her choice of nominated person.

3. The consultation requirements under the second Draft Bill would have been more onerous than those under its predecessor. They would have extended to any carer of the patient or, in the absence of such a person, to anyone else who knew the patient and with whom the AMHP considered it appropriate to consult.

4. It would have been harder to revoke the appointment of a nominated person under the 2002 Draft Bill than under the 2004 Draft Bill. Although both would have permitted the MHT to order revocation, only the latter would also have given that power to the AMHP (provided the nominated person had originally been selected by the patient). Furthermore, it would have made revocation possible on the additional, if somewhat vague, ground that the AMHP considered it 'appropriate'.

A declaration of incompatibility

1.78 By 2004, the time of the second Draft Mental Health Bill, some five years had elapsed since the UK government made its promise to the ECtHR in the *FC* case. The Government's failure to honour that promise in the intervening years led to considerable frustration within the domestic courts and, in the case of *R (M) v Secretary of State for Health*, to the High Court making a formal declaration that

124   *Ibid.*, cl 243(3)(a).
125   *Ibid.*, cl 243(3)(b).

MHA 1983, section 26 was incompatible with Article 8 of the ECHR.[126] When this case reached the ECtHR, the Government said it still proposed to honour its promise and pointed to the changes that would be made by the Mental Health Bill of 2006. It said that if the Bill did not become law, it would use another suitable legislative vehicle to rectify the incompatibility, and it pledged that this would not result in any further delay.[127]

Practicability

1.79 The Government's failure to reconcile the nearest relative provisions in MHA 1983 with the ECHR led some practitioners to adopt makeshift solutions of their own. One such was revealed in the case of *R (E) v Bristol City Council*,[128] which came before the High Court in January 2005.

1.80 At the heart of this case was the requirement, contained in section 11(4) of MHA 1983, that before making an application for a patient's detention under section 3, an ASW should consult his or her nearest relative. No such consultation need take place, however, if it is 'not reasonably practicable'.

R (E) v Bristol City Council

E had a very difficult relationship with her sister, S, who, under section 26(1) of MHA 1983, was her nearest relative. E feared that in future she might be considered for detention under section 3 of the Act, and the relevant local authority said that if that were so, its ASW would have to consult S. E said that this prospect caused her considerable distress, a fact acknowledged by her Responsible Medical Officer and agreed for the purposes of the proceedings. When the matter came to court, the judge went as far as to say: '[I]t is not in the best interests of [E] for [S] to be involved in any way with [E] and, in particular, with the assessment and/or treatment of [E]'s mental health problems'.[129]

E applied for judicial review to prevent the ASW consulting S. Referring to section 11(4) of MHA 1983, E said that in the circumstances of her case, it was not 'reasonably practicable' for an ASW to consult S and therefore, it would not be necessary for such consultation to take place.

Judgment

The High Court found for E. Under Article 8 of the ECHR, she would have a right to respect for, among other things, her private life. The court said that now that the Human Rights Act 1998 was in force, it was incumbent on all public

---

126   *R (M) v Secretary of State for Health* [2003] EWHC 1094 (Admin).
127   *M v United Kingdom.* Application no 30357/03, Decision of 13 February 2007.
128   *R (E) v Bristol City Council* [2005] EWHC 74 (Admin). See para. **1.80**.
129   *Ibid.*, at [9].

authorities to act compatibly with the ECHR. In particular, the court (which was itself a public authority) had a duty to interpret legislation in a way that was compatible with the ECHR.[130] However, the court added that there were also domestic authorities that allowed It to interpret 'reasonably practicable' in a way that would be favourable to E. The court's reasoning was as follows:

> It is important not to equate 'practicable' with 'possible'. When considering whether a course of action is *possible*, it is not permissible to consider the results of that course of action; if it can be done, it must be done. But when considering whether a course of action is *practicable* it may be permissible to look at the end result. Like so many other words in the English language, 'practicable' will take considerable colour from the context in which it is used.[131]

> The word 'practicable' is an ordinary English word of great flexibility: it takes its meaning from its context. But, whenever used, it is a call for the exercise of common sense, a warning that sound judgment will be impossible without compromise. Sometimes the context contemplates a situation rarely to be achieved, though much to be desired: the word then indicates one must be satisfied with less than perfection [...] Sometimes, [...] what the context requires may have been possible, but may not for some reason have been 'practicable'. Whatever its context, the quality of the word is that there are circumstances in which we must be content with less than 100 per cent: and it calls for judgment to determine how much less.[132]

> Practicability itself is not a black and white concept and lends itself to questions of judgment, fact and degree.[133]

The judge noted that the MHA 1983 Code of Practice suggests something rather different. In fact, it states: 'Practicability refers to the availability of the nearest relative and not to the appropriateness of informing or consulting the person concerned.'[134] To this, the judge said:

> [...] in my judgment, the Code of Practice is issued for guidance. It does not have the force of a statute. In any event, in my judgment, the passage I have quoted from above is wrong. The author, with respect, has fallen into the trap of confusing the different concepts of 'possibility' and 'practicability'. The words in paragraph 2.16 are contrary to the authorities I have referred to and, with respect, to common sense. Is the approved social worker really bound to inform/consult the nearest relative of a patient who may intensely dislike a patient and/or who would, or might, not act in the patient's best interest? The answer in, my judgment, is of course not, and particularly so where the patient,

130   Human Rights Act 1998, s 3(1).
131   *Owen and another v Crown House Engineering Limited* [1973] 3 All ER 618, *per* Griffiths J at p.621.
132   *Dedman v British Building and Engineering Appliances Ltd* [1974] 1 WLR 171, *per* Scarman LJ at p.169. See also *Re P (Adoption) (Natural Father's Rights)* [1994] 1 FLR 771, *per* Ewbank J at pp.772 and 773.
133   *R (C) v The London Maudsley NHS Trust and the Mental Health Review Tribunal* [2003] EWHC 3467 (Admin), *per* Nicholas Blake QC at [11].
134   Department of Health and Welsh Office, *Mental Health Act 1983 Code of Practice*, 1999, para. 2.16.

as here, is competent and has strongly expressed her wish that her nearest relative, [S], is not informed or consulted.[135]

Did this mean that the ASW would be relieved of his or her MHA 1983, section 11 duty? The judge said:

That, in my judgment, requires a balancing act to be performed [...]. On the one hand, Parliament clearly intended for the nearest relative of a patient to have the opportunity of playing a significant role in the protection of the patient or otherwise acting in his or her interests. [...] It is not lightly to be removed by invoking impracticability. On the other hand, to confine practicability, as does the Code of Practice, is far too restrictive and could lead and, in my judgment, would lead to positive injustice in the breach of [E]'s rights under Article 8. There is no reason to believe that an approved social worker will act otherwise than in the claimant's best interests. [E], who is competent, does not wish for [S] to carry out the functions of the relative under the Mental Health Act.[136]

1.81 The approach favoured by the judge in this case had earlier found favour with Richard Jones.[137] It had, however, been opposed by the Mental Health Act Commission, which suggested that it invests too much in the subjective views of practitioners.[138]

1.82 When required by section 11(4) of MHA 1983 to consult a nearest relative, an ASW should apply this case cautiously and only after careful deliberation. It has no general application. There will, mercifully, be few cases in which the potential consequences of consulting a nearest relative will be as grave for the patient as they were said to be in *E*. It is only where the facts are comparable that the judgment in that case will be relevant and the duty to consult might be waived.

1.83 It should also be borne in mind that the decision in *E* applies to a very restricted range of activity. Although, in an appropriate case, it might excuse an ASW from the duty of consultation, it cannot be used to deprive a nearest relative of any of his or her other rights under MHA 1983. That is so, no matter how errant the nearest relative might have been (or be said to have been). The case of *E* does not, therefore, provide a comprehensive solution to the problems identified by the ECtHR – and acknowledged by the UK Government – in the cases of *JT* and *FC*.

1.84 In fact, the case of *E* also shed a light onto the Government's latest intentions with regard to those problems. In the course of the proceedings, the court invited the Health Secretary, 'to indicate what legislative steps were being taken to meet

---

135   *R (E) v Bristol City Council* [2005] EWHC 74 (Admin), at [28].
136   *Ibid.*, at [29].
137   See, for example, Jones 2004, paras. 1–123 and 1–124.
138   Mental Health Act Commission, 2001, paras. 2.53–2.56.

the decision in *M*'. In reply, he said 'that he was actively considering the remedial legislation but that he was not in a position to say when any proposals would be put forward'.[139]

Same-sex cohabitees

1.85 There has also been legal challenge concerning the way the nearest relative provisions deal with same-sex relationships; or rather, the fact that those provisions don't deal explicitly with such relationships.

1.86 Hitherto, the same-sex partner of a detained patient enjoyed fairly restricted rights. The main problem lay with MHA 1983, section 26(6), which defines the phrase 'husband or wife'. This phrase appears in MHA 1983, section 26(1), which, of course, gives principal nearest relative rights to the person whom it describes. MHA 1983, section 26(6) allows cohabitees to qualify as the husband or wife of the patient, provided the two have lived together for at least six months. However, hitherto, the law only allowed heterosexual cohabitees to qualify under this provision.

1.87 In *Harrogate BC v Simpson*,[140] Ewbank J said: 'I agree that the expression "living together as husband and wife" [...] is not apt to include a homosexual relationship. The essential characteristic of living together as husband and wife, in my judgment, is that there should be a man and a woman.' As recently as 1999, this analysis was approved by the House of Lords.[141]

1.88 A challenge finally came in the case of *R (SSG) v Liverpool City Council and the Secretary of State for Health*,[142] which came before the High Court in October 2002.

R (SSG) v Liverpool City Council and the Secretary of State for Health

This case concerned SSG, a woman who was a lesbian, had paranoid schizophrenia and depression, and wanted her female partner, with whom she had been living since 1999, to be recognised as her nearest relative. Having at one time complied with this wish, the local authority refused to respect it, and instead purported to recognise the patient's mother, with whom she was not on good terms, as her nearest relative. The patient sought judicial review, claiming a breach of ECHR, Article 8. The local authority had some sympathy with this argument, but felt that the current law did not permit it to respect her

---

139   *R (E) v Bristol City Council* [2005] EWHC 74 (Admin), at [15].
140   *Harrogate BC v Simpson* (1985) 17 HLR 205, CA.
141   *Fitzpatrick v Sterling Housing Association Limited* [1999] 4 All ER 705.
142   *R (SSG) v Liverpool City Council and the Secretary of State for Health*, CO/1220/2002, Maurice Kay J.

wish. With the assistance of the Department of Health, the matter was concluded upon agreed terms, which were approved by Maurice Kay J.

Judgment
The terms of the agreed order included the following declaration: 'It is declared that the homosexual partner of a patient within the meaning of section 145 of the Mental Health Act 1983 can be treated as a "relative" within section 26(1) of the Mental Health Act 1983. Having regard to the specific statutory context and applying section 3 of the Human Rights Act 1998, the homosexual partner can be treated as falling within the phrase "living with the patient as the patient's husband or wife as the case may be" in section 26(6) and accordingly as a relative within section 26(1) MHA 1983.'

1.89 In its own guidance, the Department of Health has said that the consent order produced in this case 'can and should be followed by decision makers: local authorities can and should regard same sex partners as within the extended definition of husband and wife under section 26'.[143]

1.90 Therefore, provided the two partners have lived together for six months, under MHA 1983, section 26(6), one will qualify as the 'husband or wife' of the other, and therefore as his or her nearest relative under section 26(1). In this important respect, at least, MHA 1983 now gives homosexual patients rough parity with heterosexual patients – albeit the less well-favoured of heterosexual patients.[144] This too seems likely to change, for if the Government's proposed amendment is carried through, homosexuals who are parties to a civil partnership will have the right to be considered, not mere cohabitees, but as the 'husband or wife' of each other.

The new proposals

1.91 At long last, the Government has introduced its plans for MHA 1983. It no longer intends to repeal the Act and will instead content itself with a number of significant amendments.

1.92 The Mental Health Bill 2006 (MHB 2006) was introduced into the House of Lords in November 2006.[145] If carried through, it would make a number of sig-

---

143   This passage, which formerly appeared in the guidance at
       www.dh.gov.uk/PolicyAndGuidance/HealthAndSocialCareTopics/MentalHealth/MentalHealthArticle/fs/en?CONTENT
       _ID=4077674andchk=DB37MW, has now been removed.
144   See para. **2.28**.
145   Department of Health and Home Office, *Mental Health Bill*, November 2006, HL Bill 1 54/2 [MHB 2006].

nificant amendments to the nearest relative provisions in MHA 1983. Those amendments are as follows:

1. In the case of parties to a civil partnership under the terms of the Civil Partnership Act 2004, each will be the nearest relative of the other regardless of the length of their civil partnership.[146]

2. A patient him- or herself will be able to seek the appointment of an acting nearest relative.[147]

3. There will be a further ground for displacement: the nearest relative of the patient is 'not a suitable person to act as such'.[148]

4. The court will have the power to appoint as acting nearest relative, not only the person who made, or was named in, the relevant application, but, in the alternative, anyone else who, in its opinion, is a suitable person to act as such.[149]

5. The court will be able to specify the duration of any displacement order made at the patient's request.[150]

6. It will be possible in certain circumstances for a nearest relative to be displaced indefinitely.[151]

7. In some circumstances, a displaced nearest relative will need leave of the court before applying for his or her reinstatement.[152]

8. Supervised discharge, in respect of which the nearest relative has a number of rights,[153] will be replaced with Supervised Community Treatment,[154] in respect of which he or she will have none.

Comment

1.93 Some of the Government's latest proposals may be seen as less liberal – or at least less favourable to patients – than those contained in the Draft Mental Health Bill of 2002 and/or that of 2004.[155] For example:

146   *Ibid.*, cl 24. See para. **2.29**.
147   *Ibid.*, cl 21.
148   *Ibid.*, cl 21(5)(b). See also: Hansard, 17 January 2007, cols 666, 667, 670 and 671; and Joint Committee on Human Rights, Session 2006–07, Fourth report, *Legislative scrutiny: Mental Health Bill*, HL Paper 40 HC 288, 4 February 2007, paras. 30–37 and Appendix 3, paras. 23–25.
149   MHB 2006, cl 21(3).
150   *Ibid.*, cl 21(6).
151   *Ibid.*, cl 22(7).
152   *Ibid.*, cl 22(3).
153   See Chapter 6.
154   MHB 2006, cl 25–28.
155   Hewitt, 2007, p.126.

1. Even when it has been amended, MHA 1983 will give a patient no say in the initial selection of his or her nearest relative. Under the two Draft Bills, however, the patient would have made that selection. It would have been open to the AMHP to confound the patient's choice – on grounds of suitability or capacity, for example, or because regulations had been breached – but the AMHP's own discretion to appoint a nominated person would have been limited by the patient's significant power of veto.

2. Under MHA 1983, an ASW will have to consult a nearest relative about a patient's detention for treatment (or reception into guardianship), but won't have to consult the patient before recognising the nearest relative. In certain circumstances, both Draft Bills would have required the AMHP to ascertain a patient's wishes and feelings about the person who was to be appointed his or her nominated person.

3. Although the first Draft Bill contained fixed selection criteria, those criteria were a good deal more sophisticated than those in section 26 of MHA 1983. For example: they would have given a carer precedence, even if he or she wasn't a relative of the patient; and they would have made a cohabitee a patient's nominated person regardless of the length of their cohabitation. Except in the case of civil partners, even the amended MHA 1983 will not go that far.

4. The second Draft Bill dispensed with fixed selection criteria altogether, and would have given the AMHP a power that will still be denied to the ASW: simply to appoint the most suitable candidate (of those who are eligible for the role).

5. Even the first Draft Bill paid some attention to the notion of 'suitability', using it – in preference to the far cruder criterion of age – to decide between two people who would otherwise have had the same right to be appointed a patient's nominated person.

6. Both the first and (by implication) the second Draft Bills would have recognised step-relationships in a way that will continue to elude MHA 1983.

7. The power of revocation that appeared in both Draft Bills resembles that of the court under MHA 1983, which would be entitled to displace an 'unsuitable' nearest relative. The first Draft Bill, however, would have given the power of revocation, not just to the MHT, but also to the AMHP, and it set out circumstances in which he or she would have had to use that power.

2

The Nearest Relative
of an Adult

This chapter explains how, in the case of an adult, the nearest relative is to be identified.

Introduction

2.1 A person will have a 'nearest relative' if he or she is, or is *about to be*:

- detained in hospital under the Mental Health Act 1983 (MHA 1983)[1] or
- made subject to guardianship.

2.2 The following will not have a nearest relative:

- a 'restricted patient' (in other words, one detained under MHA 1983 in the course of criminal proceedings and subject to a restriction order made under section 41)[2] or
- a patient who is informal or in the community (unless he or she is *to be* made subject to MHA 1983).

2.3 The nearest relative of an adult patient is determined according to the criteria set out in section 26 of MHA 1983.[3] Where the patient is a child, different criteria apply if he or she (a) is in care, (b) has a guardian, or (c) is the subject of a residence order.[4] Otherwise, the nearest relative of a child patient is ascertained in the same way as the nearest relative of an adult patient.

---

1   But see para. **2.2**.
2   *R (H) v Mental Health Review Tribunal*, CO/2404/2000, Longmore J, 7 December 2000.
3   See Appendix 1. See also Department of Health 1995, *Mental Health Act 1983: Memorandum on Parts I to VI, VIII and X*, [MHA 1983 *Memorandum*] HMSO, para. 63.
4   See Chapter 3.

2.4 At the moment, a patient can neither choose a nearest relative nor prevent the appointment of someone he or she considers unsuitable for the role. For this reason, section 26 of MHA 1983 has become somewhat controversial.[5] The Government proposes to amend MHA 1983, so that 'unsuitable' nearest relatives can be displaced by the courts.[6]

2.5 Next of kin: A person will have no special standing under MHA 1983 simply by virtue of being a patient's 'next-of-kin'. That person may be the patient's nearest relative, but only if he or she qualifies for the role according to the criteria discussed below.

2.6 In most circumstances, it will be the responsibility of the relevant Approved Social Worker (ASW) to identify the nearest relative – for example, where a patient is to be admitted to hospital under MHA 1983. Where, however, a nearest relative has a right to information about the patient's detention, the responsibility of ensuring that he or she receives that information will be shared between the ASW and 'the managers' of the hospital concerned.[7]

2.7 Although it might be an awkward one, the job of ascertaining a patient's nearest relative need not be onerous. The nearest relative is not the person who is entitled to be recognised as such; it is the person who *appears to be* so entitled. The key question is not whether the decision-maker's view was objectively accurate, but simply whether it was reasonable.[8]

2.8 The following points should be borne in mind.

1. A patient will have only one nearest relative (although a person may be the nearest relative to more than one patient).

2. It is possible that a person will not be the nearest relative of the person who is his or her nearest relative.[9]

3. Once a nearest relative has been identified for a patient, no one else may perform the role.

4. A person determined as the nearest relative of a patient will not, however, be *obliged* to perform that role: provided the relevant formalities are observed, they may assign the role to another person.[10]

---

5   See paras. **1.15–1.21**.
6   Department of Health and Home Office, *Mental Health Bill*, November 2006, HL Bill 1 54/2 [MHB 2006], cl 21(4) and (5). See paras. **1.91** and **1.92**.
7   See paras. **5.77–5.110**.
8   See, for example, *R (WC) v South London and Maudsley NHS Trust and another* [2001] EWHC Admin 1025. See para. **2.62**.
9   See para. **2.76**.
10   See paras. **4.2–4.22**.

5. Someone may be the nearest relative of a MHA 1983 patient, even if suffering from mental disorder themselves. Provided they are capable of acting as such, their nearest relative status will not be affected.

6. Someone might be incapable of acting as nearest relative because of his or her own mental disorder, or of any other illness. That is not a reason to disregard them, but it might be a reason: (i) to seek their removal as nearest relative under section 29 of MHA 1983;[11] or (ii) to argue that it would 'impracticable' to consult them.[12]

General rules

2.9 Section 26 of MHA 1983 provides a list setting out the relatives eligible to be the nearest relative of a patient and placing them in discrete categories. It also sets out how (a) one category of relative will take precedence over another; and (b) one relative might achieve precedence over others in the same category.

2.10 It is, of course, the case that while the nearest relative will have to be a 'relative' according to the section 26 list, only one such relative can have the role at a given moment. Nevertheless, other section 26 relatives might have a part to play in the care of a someone with mental disorder: an Approved Social Worker (ASW) must, for example, have regard to their wishes when deciding whether it is necessary or proper to make an admission application or a guardianship application.[13]

2.11 Most of the list appears in section 26(1), but account must also be taken of important provisions in section 26(4) and (7) of MHA 1983. As far as a patient's nearest relative is concerned, the order of priority established by the full list might be expressed as follows:

1. any relative (see 2–9 below) (a) with whom the patient ordinarily resides[14], or (b) who provides care for the patient[15] or

2. a husband or wife (or, in some cases, a cohabitee)[16]

3. a son or daughter[17]

4. a father or mother[18]

---

11   See paras. **4.32–4.34**. At one time, this was the course advocated by the Department of Health where two detained patients were married to each other. (See Gostin 1986, para. 8.02.1.)
12   See paras. **5.48–5.56**.
13   MHA 1983, s 13(1).
14   See paras. **2.59–2.65**.
15   MHA 1983, s 26(4). See paras. **2.66–2.75**.
16   See paras. **2.17–2.22, 2.23–2.26** and **2.27–2.30**.
17   See paras. **2.31–2.40**.
18   *Ibid.*

5. a brother or sister[19]

6. a grandparent

7. a grandchild

8. an uncle or aunt

9. a nephew or niece[20]

10. anyone else with whom the patient has ordinarily resided for at least five years.[21]

2.12 In broad terms, under section 26(1) and (3) of MHA 1983, anyone in a superior category will enjoy precedence over anyone in an inferior category. This means, for example, that:

- a spouse will be the nearest relative in preference to another of the patient's relatives (unless the other relative falls within category (1) above)

- a parent will take precedence over everyone but a child, a spouse or anyone in category (1)

- a daughter will have equivalent status to a son, a mother to a father, and a sister to a brother.

Example 1

Philippa is detained under MHA 1983. She has a brother, Barry, a mother, Martha, and a son, Simon. They are her only living relatives. Ordinarily, Philippa's son, Simon, would take precedence over Martha and Barry as her nearest relative.

Example 2

Philip has two living relatives: an aunt, Agnes, and a grandmother, Gertie. Ordinarily, Gertie will take precedence over Agnes as his nearest relative, but if Philip 'ordinarily resides' with Agnes or is 'cared for' by her, it is she that will be his nearest relative.

---

19   But cf paras. **2.41** and **2.42**.
20   MHA 1983, s 26(1).
21   MHA 1983, s 26(7).

2.13 Where there is more than one person in a single section 26 category – for example, where a patient has two or more siblings – it is the elder or eldest of them that will be the nearest relative.[22]

Example 3

Pauline is unmarried, but has a son, Sid, and a brother, Brian. Her father, Felix, and her grandfather, George, are both still alive. It is Sid who will be Pauline's nearest relative because, for these purposes, a child takes precedence over a patient's sibling, father or grandfather.

Example 4

If, as well as Sid, Pauline had a second son, the older of the two would be her nearest relative.

2.14 A person related to a patient in a way not specified in the list will not qualify to be his or her nearest relative under section 26(1) and (3). This applies to any cousins or stepchildren the patient might have: in effect, their entitlement is no greater than that of someone who is in no way related to the patient. Such persons might, however, become the nearest relative if:

- they are appointed to that role by the court[23]

- the role is assigned to them by the person who is the nearest relative[24] or

- the patient 'ordinarily resides' with them and has done so for at least five years.[25]

2.15 Even if he or she would otherwise qualify under section 26, a person cannot be the nearest relative of a patient if:

- the person is under 18 years of age and neither the spouse nor a parent of the patient[26] or

- the patient is ordinarily resident in the United Kingdom, the Channel Islands or the Isle of Man, but the person is not so resident.[27]

---

22   MHA 1983, s 26(3).
23   MHA 1983, s 29. See paras. **4.23–4.95**.
24   Mental Health (Hospital, Guardianship and Consent to Treatment) Regulations 1983 [Regulations], reg 14. See: Appendix 2; paras. **4.2–4.22**.
25   MHA 1983, s 26(7). See paras. **2.59–2.65**.
26   MHA 1983, s 26(5)(c).
27   MHA 1983, s 26(5)(a).

2.16 In either of these cases, the patient's nearest relative is to be determined as if the under-age or foreign-resident person were dead.[28]

Example 5

Peter is to be detained under MHA 1983. His only relatives are: a cousin, Cecil; an uncle, Umberto; and a sister, Stephanie. Ordinarily, Peter's sister, Stephanie, would be his nearest relative. She is, however, only 17 years of age. Cecil may be disregarded, because he is not a 'relative' of Peter's for the purposes of section 26. In those circumstances, it is Umberto, as the first adult on the list, who will be Peter's nearest relative.

Example 6

If, rather than being his sister, Stephanie is Peter's *mother*, she will qualify as his nearest relative, even though she is under 18. (Parents – and spouses – under 18 years of age are an exception to the general rule.)

Example 7

It is discovered that Peter ordinarily resides with Umberto. Therefore, even if she is his mother, Stephanie will be trumped by Umberto as Peter's nearest relative. That will not be the case if Peter ordinarily resides with Cecil: Cecil is not a section 26 relative.

Husbands and wives

2.17 When determining a patient's nearest relative, his or her 'husband or wife' will usually enjoy precedence over everyone else, including any siblings, parents or grandparents the patient might have.[29] (For these purposes, a cohabitee might qualify as a patient's husband or wife.[30])

2.18 A spouse might, however, be trumped by a section 26 relative with whom the patient ordinarily resides[31] or who is their carer.[32]

2.19 A spouse under 18 years of age may be a patient's nearest relative.[33]

---

28   See paras. **2.48–2.52**.
29   MHA 1983, s 26(1) and (3).
30   See paras. **2.23–2.26** and **2.27–2.30**.
31   See paras. **2.59–2.65**.
32   See paras. **2.66–2.75**.
33   MHA 1983, s 26(5)(c).

Example 8

Paloma is married to Hector and will therefore be his nearest relative, even though he also has a brother, Bartolo, a mother, Marisa, and a grandfather, Gaspar. That will be so, even if Paloma is under 18: she will still take precedence over Gaspar, Marisa and Bartolo.

Example 9

There are two circumstances in which Bartolo might take precedence over Paloma: they are where Hector ordinarily resides with Bartolo, or where Bartolo cares for him. Alternatively, Gaspar or Marisa might become Hector's nearest relative in this way.

2.20 Where the patient is party to a polygamous marriage, the usual rule will apply, and it is the elder (or eldest) spouse who will be the nearest relative.[34]

2.21 A patient's spouse will *not* be his or her nearest relative if:

- the two are permanently separated (whether by agreement or by court order)
- one of them has deserted the other and the two remain apart.[35]

2.22 In order for one spouse to have deserted the other:

- the parties must live separately (although they might reside in the same house)
- one of them, being capable, must have formed the intention of deserting the other and must not have been justified in doing so and
- the other must not have consented to the desertion.

Example 10

Paulo is married to Wendy but having an affair with May. Wendy is ignorant of the affair: she and Paulo live together and are only occasionally apart. Wendy is Paulo's nearest relative.

Example 11

Paulo continues to see May without Wendy's knowledge. In fact, he stays at her house two nights a week, telling Wendy that he is out of town on business.

---

34   MHA 1983, s 26(3).
35   MHA 1983, s 26(5)(b).

Wendy remains his nearest relative. He is still married to Wendy and cannot be said either to have separated from her or to have deserted her. Furthermore, his relationship with May does not yet appear to be such that they can be said to be living together as husband and wife.

Example 12

Paulo tells Wendy about his affair with May. At first, little changes, and Wendy therefore remains Paulo's nearest relative. Before long, however, they begin to sleep in separate bedrooms, and eventually occupy different parts of the house. It is unlikely that one of them can be said to have deserted the other, so the key question is whether they are now separated. That will be a question of fact, based on the circumstances of the case. If – as is likely – Paulo is indeed now separated from Wendy, she will no longer be his nearest relative. It is unlikely, however, that May has become Paulo's nearest relative, because the two are not married and cannot be said to be living together as husband and wife. Paulo has a daughter, Demelza, by a previous relationship, and it is likely that she will be his nearest relative.

Example 13

Paulo moves in with May. She might become his nearest relative, but not straight away.

Cohabitees

Heterosexuals

2.23 Where a man and a woman live together as husband and wife, each is to be regarded as the husband or wife of the other (as the case may be) – and consequently his or her nearest relative – provided their cohabitation has lasted for at least six months.[36]

2.24 However, even though a man and a woman might live together as husband and wife, if one of them is married to someone else, then it is the spouse that will be the nearest relative, unless:

- the patient is permanently separated from the spouse (whether by agreement or by court order) or

- one of them has deserted the other and the two remain apart.[37]

---

36   MHA 1983, s 26(6).
37   MHA 1983, s 26(5)(b). See paras. **2.21** and **2.22**.

2.25 Whether two people are living together as husband and wife is something that will have to be determined according to the facts of each case. However, the High Court has identified the following questions, which, though they are not comprehensive, will be relevant in all cases:

- Are the two people living together in the same household?
- Do they share daily tasks and duties?
- Is there stability and a degree of permanence in their relationship?
- Does the way financial matters are handled indicate that they are cohabiting?
- Do the parties have a sexual relationship with each other?
- Are there children of the relationship?
- What is the intention (and the motivation) of the parties?

Example 14

Pauline is married to Henry but having an affair with another man, Laurence, without Henry's knowledge. She stays at Laurence's house two nights a week, telling Henry that she is out of town on business. It is unlikely that Pauline can be said to have deserted Henry, or that the two are now separated. Pauline is likely, therefore, still to be Henry's nearest relative (and *vice versa*).

Example 15

Gradually Pauline comes to spend more time with Laurence and less with Henry, and before long she is at Laurence's house as much as at the matrimonial home. Pauline remains Henry's nearest relative as long as the two are still married and haven't separated, and unless one of them deserts the other.

Example 16

The relationship between Pauline and Henry deteriorates still further. Her visits to the matrimonial home become less and less frequent. She has moved her belongings to Laurence's house and now opens a bank account with him. While no doubt of interest, and although they might in time become significant, these facts are of secondary importance in deciding whether Pauline remains Henry's nearest relative. The key question is still whether the two are now separated, or whether one can be said to have deserted the other. Unless that is so, Pauline will not cease to be Henry's nearest relative (nor he hers).

- Would a reasonable person of normal perceptions consider that the two people were cohabiting?[38]

2.26 It will be noted that although one member of a cohabiting heterosexual couple might be the other's nearest relative, he or she will have to surmount at least one obstacle – the six-month rule – that is not placed in the way of partners who are a married couple.

Example 17

Primo was married to Wynona, so that formerly each was the other's nearest relative. Ten months ago, however, they split up and Primo moved in with Carlotta. Provided the two live together as husband and wife, Carlotta will now be Primo's nearest relative (and he hers).

Example 18

If Primo split up with Wynona and moved in with Carlotta, not ten months, but three months ago, then neither woman is Primo's nearest relative: not Wynona, because, although she is his wife, the two are separated; and not Carlotta, because she has not yet lived with Primo for six months. If there is no other section 26 relative who can be said to 'care for' Primo, then any child of his, followed by a parent or sibling (etc.), will be his nearest relative.

Homosexuals

2.27 Following the *SSG* case,[39] the same rules will apply to homosexual cohabitees as apply to heterosexual cohabitees:[40] one will be the 'husband or wife' of the other, and so the nearest relative, provided:

- their cohabitation has lasted for at least six months and
- if either of them is married to another person, he or she and the other are permanently separated or one has deserted the other.

2.28 Thus, although homosexuals have been given rough parity with some heterosexuals, it is in fact with the least privileged of them: like straight people who cohabit, gay people must satisfy the six-month rule.

---

38   *Mummery v Mummery* [1942] P 107, *per* HHJ Tyrer.
39   *R (on the application of SSG) v Liverpool City Council and the Secretary of State for Health, LS (Interested party)*, CO/1220/2002. See paras. **1.88–1.90**.
40   MHA 1983, s 26(6).

Example 19

Patrick and Colin are in a homosexual relationship and have lived together for ten months. Patrick is still married to Wendy, but Colin will be his nearest relative (and he Colin's), provided that Patrick is permanently separated from Wendy, or one of them has deserted the other.

Example 20

If Patrick is *not*, as a matter of fact, separated from Wendy, or if one of them has *not* deserted the other, Wendy will still be his nearest relative, even though he is now in a relationship with Colin, and regardless of the time they have lived together.

Example 21

If Patrick and Colin have lived together, not for ten, but for two months, neither will be the nearest relative of the other. If, as a matter of fact, Patrick is separated from Wendy (or one has deserted the other), neither she nor Colin will be the nearest relative. However, provided he continues to live with Patrick (and provided Patrick and Wendy are not reconciled), Colin will become Patrick's nearest relative in another four months.

Civil partnerships

2.29 At the moment, MHA 1983 does not recognise civil partnerships under the Civil Partnership Act 2004. Consequently, one party to a civil partnership will only qualify as the 'husband or wife' of the other party, and so be his or her nearest relative, if the two have cohabited for at least six months.

The amended Act

The Government has said that it will amend section 26 of MHA 1983, so that each party to a civil partnership will be the nearest relative of the other, regardless of the length of their civil partnership.[41] This would mean that although civil partners are not regarded as such, they would enjoy at least one privilege of a married couple – a privilege that is denied to mere cohabitees.

41   MHB 2006, cl 24.

2.30 If, at the time his or her nearest relative needs to be determined, one member of a cohabiting couple is a hospital inpatient – and so might be said no longer to be living together with the other person – that other person will still be his or her nearest relative, provided the two were living together (as husband and wife) when the patient was admitted to hospital.[42] Of course, if a previous cohabitation had come to an end *before* the patient was admitted to hospital, his or her nearest relative will be determined by a different criterion. That will be so whatever the interval between the end of the cohabitation and the hospital admission.

Parents and children

2.31 In general terms, when determining a patient's nearest relative, any children he or she might have will take precedence over the patient's parents, siblings, grandparents, etc.[43]

2.32 A *child* might be 'trumped' as nearest relative by:

- a spouse of the patient[44]
- a relative with whom the patient ordinarily resides[45] or who cares for him or her.[46]

2.33 A *parent* might be 'trumped' as nearest relative by:

- a spouse of the patient[47]
- a child of the patient
- a relative with whom the patient ordinarily resides[48] or who cares for him or her.[49]

2.34 A child who is under 18 years of age:

- cannot be his or her parent's nearest relative but
- may be the nearest relative of his or her own child.[50]

---

42   MHA 1983, s 26(6).
43   MHA 1983, s 26(1) and (3).
44   See paras. **2.17–2.22, 2.23–2.26** and **2.27–2.30**.
45   See paras. **2.59–2.65**.
46   See paras. **2.66–2.75**.
47   See paras. **2.17–2.22, 2.23–2.26** and **2.27–2.30**.
48   See paras. **2.59–2.65**.
49   See paras. **2.66–2.75**.
50   MHA 1983, s 26(5)(c).

Example 22

Pazia has two relatives: a daughter, Devorah, and a nephew, Nahum. Ordinarily, Devorah would be Pazia's nearest relative, because in section 26, a patient's children take precedence over any nephews or nieces. Nahum might, however, become Pazia's nearest relative if (a) he ordinarily resides with Pazia or cares for her, or (b) Devorah is under 18.

Example 23

If Pazia – and, of course, Devorah – were under 18, that would not prevent Pazia being Devorah's nearest relative.

Illegitimacy – mother

2.35 For these purposes, an illegitimate child is to be regarded as the legitimate child of his or her mother.[51] This means, for example, that where a single woman has two sons, one of whom is legitimate and one illegitimate, both sons are equally entitled to be considered for the role and it is simply the elder of the two that will be the nearest relative.

Illegitimacy – father

2.36 An illegitimate child might also be regarded as the legitimate child of his or her father, but only if the father has 'parental responsibility' for him or her.[52] Where a father does not have parental responsibility for his illegitimate child, he will not be a relative for the purposes of section 26. He might, however, *become* the child's nearest relative:

- by being appointed to the role by the court[53]

- by having the role assigned to him by someone who *is* the nearest relative[54] or

- if the child patient ordinarily resides with him and has done so for at least five years.[55]

---

51   MHA 1983, s 26(2)(a).
52   MHA 1983, s 26(2)(b). See para. **2.37**.
53   MHA 1983, s 29. See paras. **4.23–4.95**.
54   Regulations, reg 14. See: Appendix 2; paras. **4.2–4.22**.
55   MHA 1983, s 26(7). See paras. **2.59–2.65**.

Parental responsibility

2.37 This is governed by the Children Act 1989.[56] In broad terms:

- A mother will have parental responsibility for her child.[57]

- A father will have parental responsibility for his child if he was married to the mother when the child was born,[58] or if he marries the mother subsequently (in which case the child will be said to be 'legitimated').[59]

- Where the father is not married to the mother, he might *acquire* parental responsibility, but only if: (a) he becomes registered as the child's father (and the birth itself was registered on or after 1 December 2003); (b) he makes a 'parental responsibility agreement' with the mother; (c) the court orders that he should have such responsibility;[60] or (d) he becomes the child's guardian, either by order of the court,[61] or by agreement with the mother or another guardian.[62]

- A step-parent might acquire parental responsibility for a child, either (a) by agreement with those who already have such responsibility or (b) by order of the court.[63]

- Where, although he is not married to the mother, the father has parental responsibility for a child, he will lose it: (a) if the court makes an order to that effect;[64] (b) when the child reaches 18 years of age;[65] or (c) if the child is adopted.[66]

Example 24

Padraig and Shauna never married and are now living apart. They have two children: a son, Sean, who is 16, and a daughter, Deirdre, who is ten. Sean is to be detained under MHA 1983. Padraig is older than Shauna, but she will be Sean's nearest relative unless Padraig has parental responsibility for him.

---

56   See Appendix 1.
57   Children Act 1989, s 2(1) and (2).
58   Children Act 1989, s 2(1).
59   Legitimacy Act 1976, s 2.
60   Children Act 1989, s 4(1).
61   Children Act 1989, s 5(1). See paras. **3.11–3.17**.
62   Children Act 1989, s 5(3) and (4). See paras. **3.11–3.17**.
63   Children Act 1989, s 4A(1).
64   Children Act 1989, s 4(2A) and (3).
65   Children Act 1989, s 91(7) and (8).
66   Adoption Act 1976, s 12(1).

Example 25

Padraig and Shauna resume their cohabitation. Shauna remains Sean's nearest relative.

Example 26

Eventually, and for the first time, Padraig and Shauna get married. At that point, Sean is 'legitimated' and Padraig is treated as his father. As Padraig is older than Shauna, he will supplant her as Sean's nearest relative.

Stepchildren

2.38 A step-relationship is not one of those set out in the section 26(1) list. This means that if the stepchild of a patient is to be his or her nearest relative, the step-child will have to:

- qualify as a *non*-relative (by having ordinarily resided with the patient for at least five years)[67]
- be appointed to that role by the court[68] or
- have the role assigned to him or her by whoever currently is the nearest relative.[69]

Adopted children

2.39 An adopted child is to be treated as the child of his or her adoptive parents.[70] Therefore, where it is necessary to determine the nearest relative of either parent, the adopted child will enjoy the same right to be considered as any natural child enjoys.

Example 27

Penelope has four children: two sons, Scott and Sheldon, by her first husband, Frank; and two daughters, Daisy and Darlene, by her second husband, Hank. As both Frank and Hank are now dead, and because Penelope has no other relatives, the eldest of her children will be her nearest relative.

---

67   See MHA 1983, s 26(7). See paras. **2.53–2.58** and **2.59–2.65**.
68   MHA 1983, s 29. See paras. **4.23–4.93**.
69   Regulations, reg 14. See: Appendix 2; paras. **4.2–4.22**.
70   Adoption and Children Act 2002, s 46(2).

Example 28

In fact, further enquiries reveal that although Penelope regarded Daisy and Darlene as her own children, their mother was in fact Hank's first wife. Therefore, as the two girls are her stepchildren, neither of them can qualify as her nearest relative, and it is to the elder of her sons, Scott and Sheldon, that that role will fall.

Example 29

Yet further enquiries reveal that Penelope adopted Daisy and Darlene two years ago. In those circumstances, they fall into the same section 26(1) category as Scott and Sheldon, and the eldest of the four will be Penelope's nearest relative.

Example 30

Scott is the eldest of the four children and would therefore be Penelope's nearest relative. For the last couple of weeks, however, Darlene has been caring for her. If the nature and degree of that care is sufficient, Darlene will trump Scott as Penelope's nearest relative. (If she were not Penelope's adopted daughter but her stepdaughter, Darlene could not gain precedence in this way – unless the role was transferred to her by the court or the rightful nearest relative, she would only acquire it by ordinarily residing with Penelope for at least five years.)

Children in care, etc.

2.40   Different considerations apply in the case of children (a) who are in care, (b) for whom a guardian has been appointed, or (c) who are the subject of a residence order.[71] In broad terms, the nearest relative:

- of a *child in care* is the local authority[72]

- of a *child with a guardian* is the guardian[73]

- of a *child who is the subject of a residence order* is the person named in that order.[74]

71   See Chapter 3.
72   MHA 1983, s 27.
73   MHA 1983, s 28.
74   *Ibid.*

Half-siblings

2.41 When dealing with half-siblings, MHA 1983 says two things that might at first appear contradictory. First, it says that when applying section 26, 'any relationship of the half-blood shall be treated as a relationship of the whole blood'.[75] Later, however, the Act talks of 'relatives of the whole blood being preferred to relatives of the same description of the half-blood'.[76]

2.42 In fact, these provisions can be reconciled, and they may be summarised as follows:

- the half-sibling of a patient will qualify to be his or her nearest relative in the same way as a full sibling but

- where the patient has both a full sibling and a half-sibling, the former will take precedence over the latter.

Example 31

Peter has two surviving relatives: his grandmother, Gladys, and a half-brother, Henry. In this case, the fact that Henry is not Peter's full brother is immaterial: he will be entitled to be considered under MHA 1983 in the same way that a full brother would have been. In fact, Henry will be Peter's nearest relative, because section 26(1) gives a sibling (or half-sibling) precedence over a grandparent.

Example 32

If, as well as his half-brother, Peter has a full brother, Simon, it is Simon that will be his nearest relative, because, when a choice must be made between two relatives in the same class, one of the whole blood is to be preferred to one of the half-blood.

Other relatives

2.43 Where there is a relative who (a) ordinarily resides with the patient[77] or (b) cares for him or her,[78] that relative will take precedence over everyone else in the section 26(1) list and will therefore be the patient's nearest relative. This applies even if the patient also has, for example, a spouse or a child, a parent or a sibling.[79] In such

---

75   MHA 1983, s 26(2).
76   MHA 1983, s 26(3).
77   See paras. **2.59–2.65**.
78   See paras. **2.66–2.75**.
79   MHA 1983, s 26(4).

a case, there is no minimum period of residence or care before the relative might qualify as the nearest relative.[80]

2.44 For these purposes, a person will be a patient's 'relative' if their relationship is one of those set out in the section 26(1) list. This means that a mere cousin or stepchild of the patient will not come within this provision.[81] If such a person is to qualify as the patient's nearest relative, he or she will have to do so as a *non*-relative (in other words, by having ordinarily resided with the patient for at least five years).[82] (Alternatively, of course, he or she might have the role of nearest relative assigned to him or her or be appointed to that role by the court.)

2.45 If more than one relative meets either of these conditions, the elder or eldest of them will be the nearest relative.[83]

Example 33

Patricia has a husband, Hubert, and a son, Steve. For the last six years, however, she has resided with her niece, Nadia. It is Nadia who will be Patricia's nearest relative, and it makes no difference that Patricia has a husband and a son. The length of her residence with Nadia is also irrelevant: provided Patricia was *ordinarily* resident with her, Nadia would have been the nearest relative if it had been for one year, or one month, or one day. The same would have been true if, rather than the two residing together, Nadia had provided care to Patricia.

2.46 When it becomes necessary to determine his or her nearest relative, a patient might be in hospital and therefore no longer residing with any other person (or residing with a whole ward-full of them). In those circumstances, the relative with whom the patient ordinarily resided, or who cared for him or her, immediately before he or she came into hospital will be the nearest relative.[84] If, at the time of being admitted to hospital, the patient was neither ordinarily residing with, nor being cared for by, a relative, the nearest relative will be determined by criteria other than these.

2.47 Where a person, A, is the nearest relative of a relative, Z, as a result of providing care to him or her, Z will not necessarily be A's own nearest relative. MHA 1983

---

80   The position is different in the case of *non*-relatives with whom a patient ordinarily resides or who care for him or her. See paras. **2.53–2.58** and **2.59–2.65**.
81   See para. **2.38**.
82   See MHA 1983, s 26(7).
83   MHA 1983, s 26(3).
84   MHA 1983, s 26(4).

does not state that any nearest relative relationship will be symmetrical, and A may well have a section 26 relative who is closer to him or her than Z.[85]

Relatives living abroad

2.48 Where a person who would otherwise be the nearest relative is ordinarily resident[86] outside the United Kingdom, the Channel Islands or the Isle of Man, it is necessary to consider the whereabouts of the patient:

- if the patient is ordinarily resident in the UK, the Channel Islands or Isle of Man, no expatriate relative can be his or her nearest relative (and is to be treated for that purpose as if he or she were dead)[87]

- if the patient is not so resident, a person may qualify as nearest relative even though he or she is ordinarily resident outside the UK, the Channel Islands or Isle of Man.[88]

2.49 For these purposes, the United Kingdom is Great Britain (which consists of England, Wales and Scotland) and Northern Ireland.[89]

2.50 The concept of ordinary residence is discussed below.[90] It will have to be considered afresh according to the facts of each case.

2.51 It seems that it might take longer for a person to be regarded as ordinarily resident in a country than in a town. In a child care case, Lord Brandon said, in a slightly different context:

A person may cease to be habitually resident in country A in a single day if he or she leaves it with a settled intention not to return to it but to take up long-term residence in country B instead. Such a person cannot, however, become habitually resident in country B in a single day. An appreciable period of time and a settled intention will be necessary to enable him or her to become so. During that appreciable period of time the person will have ceased to be habitually resident in country A but not yet have become habitually resident in country B.[91]

2.52 A relative who is ordinarily resident within the UK does not cease to be so if he or she goes on holiday, no matter that the holiday might be a long one.

---

85   See para. **2.76**.
86   See paras. **2.59–2.65**.
87   MHA 1983, s 26(5)(a).
88   See Mental Health Act Commission, *Nearest Relatives of non-UK Residents*, 17 July 2006 –
        www.mhac.org.uk/Pages/documents/guidance_notes/Nearest_relatives_of_non-uk_residents.pdf
89   Interpretation Act 1978, s 5 and Sched 1.
90   See paras. **2.59–2.65**.
91   *C v S (A Minor) (Abduction)* [1990] 2 FLR 442 at 454, HL.

Example 34

Philippa lives alone. She has two surviving relatives: Reginald, who, like her, lives in Manchester; and Ricardo, who lives in Lisbon. Reginald is Philippa's uncle, and Ricardo, her brother. Although, as Philippa's brother, Ricardo would come first on any list drawn up under section 26(1) of MHA 1983, it is Reginald who will be her nearest relative. Ricardo must be disregarded, because, while Philippa lives in the UK, he does not.

Example 35

It would still be necessary to disregard Ricardo, even if Reginald did not exist. The result would be that Philippa had no nearest relative.

Example 36

If Philippa lived, not in Manchester, but with her brother Ricardo in Lisbon, Ricardo would be her nearest relative (if she were to come to England and need to be detained under MHA 1983).

Other people

2.53   A person who, though not the patient's relative, has 'ordinarily resided' with him or her for at least five years will be included on the section 26 list, but (a) will come last on that list and (b) will not trump any spouse of the patient unless the two are permanently separated or one has deserted the other.[92]

Example 37

Preston has only one relative, his brother, Humphrey, who will be his nearest relative. For the last three years, however, Preston has lived with Fiona, who has been his friend since they were both children. Even though Humphrey ranks higher than her on the section 26 list, Fiona may in future become Preston's nearest relative, but only if the two continue to live together for another two years. In the interim, Humphrey will remain Preston's nearest relative.

Example 38

If, rather than his friend, Fiona was Preston's niece, the length of time she had resided with him would be irrelevant; she would already be his nearest relative.

---

92   MHA 1983, s 26(7), read with s 26(5)(b). See para. **2.22**.

2.54 As noted above,[93] a 'relative' for these purposes does not include a person related to the patient in a way not specified in the section 26(1) list. The *ordinary residence* rule is the only way such a person might qualify under section 26 to be the patient's nearest relative. (That person would not be able to achieve a similar result by providing care to the patient.) However, and as also noted above, the person might alternatively become the patient's nearest relative:

- by being appointed to that role by the court[94]
- by having the role assigned to him or her by the person who is currently the nearest relative.[95]

2.55 The five-year period will have to have been continuous, and it is considered to remain so where the patient and the person with whom he or she ordinarily resides are temporarily separated (for example, during a holiday).

Example 39

If, in example 37 above, Preston goes abroad for a fortnight without Fiona, that won't break the continuity of their residence together. If, however, the foreign sojourn lasts for six months, and if, rather than a holiday, its purpose is a business trip, it is likely that Preston and Fiona will be said no longer ordinarily to reside together.

2.56 If, at the time his or her nearest relative needs to be determined, a patient is a hospital inpatient, and therefore no longer residing with any other person (whether 'ordinarily' or otherwise), any non-relative with whom he or she had ordinarily resided for five years immediately before coming into hospital will be the nearest relative.[96] If the patient was not ordinarily residing with anyone, then his or her nearest relative will be determined by a criterion other than this one.

2.57 It has been suggested that where a patient lives communally with others – in a religious community, for example, or a care home – he or she might be said ordinarily to reside with all of them, so that, if no one else qualifies under section 26, the oldest of those others might qualify as the nearest relative.[97] Although this suggestion might seem outlandish, it is probably correct, if only from a strictly

---

93 See para. **2.14**.
94 MHA 1983, s 29. See paras. **4.23–4.95**.
95 Regulations, reg. 14. See: Appendix 2; paras. **4.2–4.22**.
96 MHA 1983, s 26(4).
97 Jones 2004, paras. 1–421.

legal perspective. Much will depend upon the nature of the living arrangements and the extent to which they are truly shared.

Example 40

Piotr lives with his wife, Wendy, in a kibbutz in the Peak District. All members of the kibbutz have equal access to its facilities and share tasks equally. If, in Piotr's case, the oldest member of the kibbutz were to be accorded a place on the section 26 list, it would be as a result of his or her ordinarily residing with Piotr. While his wife Wendy remained with Piotr, however, she would always be his nearest relative. Furthermore, any other relatives of Piotr's would always have precedence over the oldest member of the kibbutz.

2.58 Where, by virtue of the ordinary residence provisions, a patient acquires a nearest relative who is unwilling – or feels unable – adequately to perform the role, the nearest relative might be invited to assign the role to someone else.[98] If a nearest relative is incapable of acting as such by reason either of mental disorder or of another illness, an application might be made for an order transferring the role to someone else.[99] It might be argued that, pending such transfer, it would not be reasonably practicable to consult the outgoing nearest relative about the patient's admission to hospital or to guardianship under MHA 1983.[100]

Ordinarily resident

2.59 As we have seen, the notion of ordinary residence is an important one in the context of the nearest relative. In summary:

- A relative who 'ordinarily resides' with a patient will probably be his or her nearest relative (as will one who 'cares for' the patient).[101]

- A person who, though not a relative, has ordinarily resided with the patient for at least five years will fall within section 26, but (a) will come last on the list and (b) will not enjoy precedence over a spouse of the patient, unless the spouses are permanently separated or one has deserted the other.[102]

---

98   Regulations, reg 14. See: Appendix 2; paras. **4.2–4.22**.
99   MHA 1983, s 29(3). See paras. **4.32–4.34**.
100   MHA 1983, s 11(4). See paras. **5.48–5.56**.
101   MHA 1983, s 26(4).
102   MHA 1983, s 26(7), read with s 26(5)(b). See paras. **2.53–2.58**.

- A person who is not ordinarily resident in the UK cannot be the nearest relative of a patient who *is* so resident.[103]

2.60 Although MHA 1983 does not define 'ordinarily resides', a number of cases have examined what it might mean. It is clear, first of all, that there is no hard-and-fast rule, and that each case should be decided on its own merits.[104]

2.61 The classic definition of 'ordinarily resident' was given by Lord Scarman in the *Shah* case. He 'unhesitatingly' said:

> [It] refers to a man's abode in a particular place or country[,] which he has adopted voluntarily and for settled purposes as part of the regular order of his life for the time being, whether short or long duration.[105]

2.62 This definition was accepted and applied in the case of *WC*,[106] although the result in that case was that the patient's nearest relative was found to be his wife, even though he had been residing with his mother immediately before he was admitted to hospital.[107] It seems that there need not be a 'right' answer in this regard, or at least, that if there is a right answer, the ASW is not bound to find it. In *WC*, the court said:

> Under the provisions of section 11(3) the [ASW] is not obliged to resolve this legal issue as to ordinary residence so as to get it right in absolute terms. What matters is who *appears to him* to be the nearest relative in the context of the rules set out in the relevant provisions of the Mental Health Act.[108]

2.63 More recently, Lord Slynn has suggested that a person's ordinary residence is 'a place where at the relevant time [he or she] in fact resides'.[109] Furthermore:

> So long as that place where he eats and sleeps is voluntarily accepted by him, the reason why he is there rather than somewhere else does not prevent that place from being his normal residence. He may not like it, he may prefer some other place, but that place is for the relevant time the place where he [ordinarily] resides. If a person, having no other accommodation, takes his few belongings and moves into a barn for a period to work on a farm[,] that is where during that period he is normally resident, however much he might prefer some more better or permanent accommodation.[110]

---

103   MHA 1983, s 26(5).
104   *Mohammed v Hammersmith and Fulham LBC* [2002] UKHL 57, *per* Lord Slynn at [18].
105   *Shah v Barnet LBC* [1983] 1 All ER 226, HL, at p.235.
106   R *(WC) v South London and Maudsley NHS Trust and another* [2001] EWHC Admin 1025.
107   See Bartlett and Sandland 2003, pp.202–203.
108   R *(WC) v South London and Maudsley NHS Trust and another* [2001] EWHC Admin 1025, *per* Scott Baker J at [12] [emphasis added].
109   *Mohammed v Hammersmith and Fulham LBC* [2002] UKHL 57, at [18].
110   *Ibid.*

2.64 In one case, the parties were in dispute as to whether a patient might be said to be ordinarily resident with his parents, whose home he had left after a disagreement, or at his grandmother's house, where he had sought refuge. The court refused to see these as the only alternatives, and said that those responsible for determining the patient's nearest relative

> should have considered also the possibility that he may not have been ordinarily resident anywhere[,] and [they] should have specifically asked themselves – bearing in mind [the patient's] itinerant lifestyle, his lack of stability and the condition of his mental health – whether he really had settled down sufficiently at his grandmother's for her home to be regarded as his place of ordinary residence.[111]

2.65 It would appear, therefore, that the following propositions are true.

- The place in which a patient is ordinarily resident is to be determined afresh in every case.

- There is no hard-and-fast rule.

- Everything will depend on where, as a question of fact, the patient is living (and eating and sleeping) at a particular time, and whether he or she has voluntarily accepted it as such.

- This is so, even if the patient would prefer it to be – or will eventually go – somewhere else.

- There might be no place in which a patient is ordinarily resident (in which case, the nearest relative will be determined otherwise than by this provision).

Example 41

Patrice has two living relatives, his niece, Naomi (who is 35) and his nephew, Nigel (33). Ordinarily, as the elder of his only relatives, Naomi would be Patrice's nearest relative. For the last two years, however, Patrice has resided with Nigel, who is therefore his nearest relative.

Example 42

Patrice and Nigel have a violent row, and Patrice leaves the house in a state of great anger and spends the night in a bus shelter. If, having quit Nigel's house, Patrice intends not to return to it, it is likely that he is no longer ordinarily resident with Nigel, and that Nigel has therefore ceased to be his nearest relative. In such circumstances, Patrice might have no ordinary residence, so

---

111   *R v Liverpool City Council, ex parte F*, CO/2744/96, 16 April 1997, *per* McCullough J.

that Naomi, being the older of his only two relatives, would be his nearest relative. If Patrice's intentions *vis-à-vis* Nigel are less settled, it might be that the latter remains his nearest relative.

Example 43

Patrice spends the next night at the home of his good friend, Fawn. It might be too early to conclude that he is 'ordinarily' resident with her. The following day, however, Patrice goes back to Nigel's house to pick up his possessions, and when he gets back to Fawn's house he says, 'I feel this is where I belong'. It is possible that he is now ordinarily resident with Fawn, and that possibility will increase the longer he spends there. As she is not a relative of Patrice's, however, Fawn will only have a chance of becoming his nearest relative if their arrangement lasts for five years (or if, within that period, they live together as husband and wife for at least six months). In the interim, as Nigel has lost it and Fawn not yet attained it, it seems the role of Patrice's nearest relative will revert to Naomi.

Cared for

2.66 Where a patient is 'cared for' by a relative, that relative will take precedence over all other relatives as the nearest relative, even if the patient has a spouse.[112]

Example 44

Pedro has three living relatives: a son, Sebastian, whom he doesn't see from one month to the next; a niece, Nora, who cleans for him once a week; and a cousin, Christopher, who brings him his meals every day. Christopher is older than Nora, but if the only way he might qualify is by virtue of the care he provides, he will not be Pedro's nearest relative. This is because Christopher is Pedro's cousin, and their relationship is not one of those described in section 26 of MHA 1983. Nora's relationship with Pedro is that of niece and uncle, which *is* described in section 26. Therefore, if she can be said to provide care for Pedro, Nora will be his nearest relative, and she will overreach Sebastian. (The same would be true if Pedro had a wife.)

2.67 Though the relevant provision in MHA 1983 gives such precedence to anyone 'the patient ordinarily resides with or is cared for by', it is not the case that

---

112   MHA 1983, s 26(4).

someone who cares for him or her must do so 'ordinarily' (for that word qualifies 'resides' and not 'cared for by').[113]

2.68 The words 'cared for' are not defined by MHA 1983, but they have been interpreted by the courts. In the case of *Re D*,[114] the Court of Appeal held:

- they are clear and everyday words
- when seeking to apply them, an ASW must act in a pragmatic and common sense manner
- if a relative is to be considered the nearest relative under this provision, the services he or she provides need not have been provided over a long period, but they must be 'more than minimal'.

2.69 In *Re D*, the services provided by the relative were sufficient to make her the nearest relative. She assisted the patient to manage his financial affairs, often paying his expenses out of her own pocket, checked whether he was eating properly and cooked for him when she thought he was not, and cleaned his soiled clothes and bedlinen.

2.70 In the case of *F*, McCullough J said that when seeking to ascertain whether a relative has cared for a patient,

> [I]t will be necessary to take into account the duration, continuity and quality of the care afforded by the relative under consideration as having assumed the role [...] and also the intention of the patient himself.[115]

2.71 It would appear, therefore, that the following propositions are true.

- Whether or not a patient is cared for – and if so, by whom – is to be determined afresh in every case.
- There is no hard-and-fast rule.
- The words are to be taken in their normal, everyday sense.
- The services provided by the relative must be more than minimal, but they needn't have been provided over a long period.
- However, the services will have to have about them a quality of continuity.
- The intention of the patient is likely to be relevant.

113   *Re D (Mental Patient: Habeas Corpus)* [2000] 2 FLR 848.
114   *Ibid.*
115   *R v Liverpool City Council, ex parte F*, CO/2744/96, 16 April 1997.

Example 45

Gareth is hoping to be acknowledged as the nearest relative of his grandfather, Philip. Unfortunately for Gareth, Philip also has a wife, Wilhelmina, and 11 children. Gareth, however, will point to the fact that he collects Philip's newspaper every morning. Gareth also washes, dresses and feeds his grandfather every day and cleans his house on Thursdays. In those circumstances (and provided he is over 18 years of age), it is likely that Gareth will be Philip's nearest relative. This is so especially as Philip calls his grandson 'my carer' and Gareth has ordered a new mop to help in his cleaning duties.

2.72 Where the care provided is sufficient to make its provider the nearest relative of the patient, but it is provided by more than one person, the elder (or eldest) of the carers will in fact be the nearest relative.

2.73 Special care should be taken to ensure that two (or more) people are not regarded as joint carers where, in fact, one of them provides a disproportionate share of the patient's care. The fact that the two (or more) proportions are not identical might, however, be irrelevant, unless they differ so greatly that one person might not, in truth, be said to care for his or her relative at all.

Example 46

Polly has four children: Catherine, who is 26, Carl (24), Claudia (22) and Clive (20). Polly's husband died last year. Ordinarily, therefore, it would be Catherine, as the eldest child, who would be Polly's nearest relative. However, the children now take it in turns to care for their mother:
- Catherine on Monday
- Carl on Tuesday and Wednesday
- Claudia on Thursday
- Clive on Friday, Saturday and Sunday.

The care provided is the same every day. It is likely that Catherine will remain Polly's nearest relative. Section 26 gives the role to a relative who provides care for a patient; not to the relative who provides the *most* care. Where two or more relatives come within the same section 26 category – for example, by each providing care to the patient – there is but one way of distinguishing between them: the elder or eldest of them will be the nearest relative.

Example 47

If the tasks undertaken for Polly by Catherine are minimal when compared with those undertaken by her siblings, it might not be possible to say that she cares for Polly, and she might not, therefore, be entitled to the degree of precedence afforded to Carl, Claudia and Clive. In those circumstances, the eldest member of this trio – Carl – would be Polly's nearest relative.

Example 48

If, in truth, the care provided for Polly by her children is no more than minimal, her nearest relative will be Catherine, not by virtue of the care she provides (for she provides none), but simply because she is the oldest child.

2.74 Where a patient is cared for by one relative but ordinarily resides with another, either of the two might qualify as nearest relative, and it is to the elder of them that the role will fall.

Example 49

Clarrie is 97 and her husband, Henry, is 99. Henry lives in a care home and is unable to care for Clarrie, so she lives with her son, Sid. He, however, works during the day, so the job of caring for Clarrie falls to her daughter Dottie (Sid's sister). Either Sid or Dottie might qualify as Clarrie's nearest relative: Sid because his mother ordinarily resides with him, and Dottie because she provides care for her mother. As is usual in these situations, the role will fall to the elder of the two. That is Dottie, and the fact that she cares for her mother will entitle her to precedence over Henry, Clarrie's spouse as the nearest relative.

2.75 If the person caring for a patient is not a relative (as that term is understood in section 26 of MHA 1983) the care he or she gives will not enable him or her to qualify as the patient's nearest relative.

Example 50

If, in example 51, Dottie were not Clarrie's daughter, but her stepdaughter, she would not be the nearest relative, and that role would fall to Sid (just as would happen if Dottie were merely the daughter of a friend of Clarrie's). This is because, for the purpose of section 26, a stepchild is not the 'relative' of a patient, and it is only by being a relative that someone who cares for a patient can become his or her nearest relative. If, however, the step-relationship were between Sid and Clarrie, Sid would still qualify as her nearest relative, because a non-relative can accede to the position where, rather than merely provide care, he or she ordinarily resides with the patient.

Asymmetrical relationships

2.76 MHA 1983 does not state that where one person is the nearest relative of another, the arrangement will be reciprocal. The following are examples of such asymmetrical relationships.

- A is the nearest relative of Z, his relative, because he provides care for her. As far as A's nearest relative is concerned, however, the care he provides for Z is irrelevant. If Z is the first of his relatives according to section 26, she will be his nearest relative; but if another relative ranks higher in the list, Z will be overreached.

- B is Y's aunt and also, because Y has no closer relatives, his nearest relative. B, however, has a number of closer relatives, including a son and a daughter. It is the older of them that will be her nearest relative.

3

The Nearest Relative
of Some Minors

This chapter sets out the special rules that apply where it is necessary to ascertain the nearest relative of certain minors.

Introduction

3.1 With three exceptions, the rules for determining the nearest relative of a patient who is – or is to be – subject to the Mental Health Act 1983 (MHA 1983) are the same, whether the patient is over or under 18 years of age.[1] The exceptions relate to certain minors.

3.2 The minors to whom those different rules apply are:

1. children and young persons in care[2]

2. minors that are subject to guardianship under the Children Act 1989[3]

3. minors that are wards of court.[4]

Children and young persons in care

3.3 Where a child or young person is in care, the nearest relative is to be determined according to the provisions of section 27 of MHA 1983. The effect of those provisions is that in certain circumstances, section 26 – by which the nearest relative would otherwise be determined – will have no application.

3.4 The circumstances in which section 27 of MHA 1983 will apply are where the patient is a child or young person and:

---

1   See Chapter 2.
2   See paras. **3.3–3.10**.
3   See paras. **3.11–3.17**.
4   MHA 1983, s 33. See Appendix 1.

1. he or she is in the care of the local authority by virtue of a care order within the meaning of the Children Act 1989[5] or

2. the rights and powers of his or her parent are vested in the local authority by virtue of section 16 of the Social Work (Scotland) Act 1968.[6]

3.5 In either of these circumstances:

1. the nearest relative of the patient will be the relevant local authority unless

2. the patient is married, in which case the nearest relative will be the patient's spouse.

3.6 This provision will apply only in the case of someone who is both a 'child' and a 'patient' within the meaning of MHA 1983.

- A 'child' is defined in the Children Act 1989 as a person under the age of 18 years.[7] This means, in effect, that the term 'a young person' is redundant: it cannot signify a person older than a 'child' – in other words, over 18 years of age – and this provision cannot be meant to apply to such a person.

- A patient is 'a person suffering or appearing to be suffering from mental disorder'.[8]

3.7 In the Children Act, the definition of 'care order' includes an interim care order made under section 38 of that Act.[9]

3.8 As we have seen,[10] the term 'husband or wife' has been defined quite broadly:

- both by MHA 1983 itself, which in section 26 says that it includes cohabitees[11] and

- by the courts, which have accepted that homosexual cohabitees might qualify as the 'husband or wife' of each other – and therefore, as each other's nearest relative – on the same basis as heterosexual cohabitees.[12]

3.9 It is not clear whether – and if so, how far – these expanded definitions apply in the case of children (and young persons) who fall within section 27 of MHA 1983. However, the following points should be noted.

---

5   MHA 1983, s 27(a). See Appendix 1.
6   MHA 1983, s 27(b). See Appendix 1.
7   Children Act 1989, s 105(1).
8   MHA 1983, s 145(1).
9   Children Act 1989, s 31(11).
10   See paras. **2.17–2.22**.
11   MHA 1983, s 26(6).
12   *R (SSG) v Liverpool City Council and the Secretary of State for Health, LS (Interested party)*, CO/1220/2002.

1. In stating that two cohabitees might (eventually) qualify as each other's nearest relative, section 26 of MHA 1983 states in terms that that is so 'in this section'. This suggests that the provision is not to apply in other sections of MHA 1983, and not, therefore, in section 27.

2. In finding as it did concerning homosexual cohabitees, the court was simply seeking to achieve parity, not between homosexuals and heterosexuals generally, but between *cohabitees* of those respective persuasions. It did not feel the need to ensure that mere cohabitees enjoyed the same rights as married partners.

3.10 This suggests:

1. that a local authority's claim to be the nearest relative of a patient under section 27 of MHA 1983 will not be defeated by a mere cohabitee of the patient (even one who has enjoyed that status for more than six months)

2. that homosexual cohabitees are unlikely to enjoy the same rights under section 27 of MHA 1983 that they enjoy under section 26 and

3. until section 26 of MHA 1983 is amended, and unless, when amended, it places civil partners on the same footing as married people, a child who enters into a civil partnership will have no greater right in this regard than an adult who does the same: he or she will only be his or her partner's nearest relative if the two have cohabited for at least six months. (A person may enter into a civil partnership once he or she has attained the age of 16 years.[13])

Minors subject to guardianship

3.11 Where a child or young person is subject to the guardianship under the Children Act 1989, the nearest relative is to be determined according to the provisions of section 28 of MHA 1983. The effect of those provisions is, again, that in certain circumstances, section 26 will have no application.

3.12 Those circumstances are where the patient is a person under 18 years of age:

1. for whom a guardian has been appointed (under section 5 of the Children Act 1989)[14] or

---

13   Civil Partnership Act 2004, s 3(1).
14   MHA 1983, s 28(1)(a). See Appendix 1.

2. in respect of whom there is a residence order (under section 8 of the Children Act 1989).[15]

3.13 Only a guardian appointed for a patient under section 5 of the Children Act will become his or her nearest relative in this way.[16] A person appointed the patient's guardian under MHA 1983 will not qualify as the nearest relative under section 28. That person might, however, still qualify as the patient's nearest relative:

- by being appointed under the Children Act as well
- by being named in a residence order or
- by virtue of section 26 of MHA 1983.[17]

3.14 In these circumstances, the nearest relative of the child-patient will be (a) the guardian or (b) the person named in the residence order (as appropriate).

3.15 If there is more than one guardian, or if more than one person is named in a residence order, they will share the role of nearest relative and enjoy equal powers. (This position may be contrasted with the one that obtains in cases covered by section 26 of MHA 1983, according to which a patient can have only one nearest relative.)

3.16 A person who would otherwise qualify as the nearest relative of a patient under this provision will not do so if:

1. unlike the patient, he or she is not ordinarily resident in the United Kingdom, the Channel Islands or the Isle of Man[18]

2. he or she is the spouse of the patient, but is permanently separated from him or her, either by agreement or under an order of a court[19]

3. he or she has deserted or been deserted by the patient for a period that has not yet come to an end[20] or

4. not being the spouse or parent of the patient, he or she is under 18 years of age.[21]

3.17 In section 28 there is no equivalent of the provision in section 27 to the effect that the husband or wife of a child-patient in care (etc.) will take precedence over the local authority as his or her nearest relative.[22] Where a minor is subject to

---

15   MHA 1983, s 28(1)(b). See Appendix 1.
16   MHA 1983, s 7.
17   See para. **2.9** *et seq.*
18   MHA 1983, ss 28(2) and 26(5)(a). The notion of 'ordinary residence' is discussed in paras. **2.59–2.65**.
19   MHA 1983, ss 28(2) and 26(5)(b). See also para. **2.21**.
20   *Ibid.*
21   MHA 1983, ss 28(2) and 26(5)(c).
22   See para. **3.5**.

guardianship under the Children Act 1989, no spouse of his or hers will enjoy such precedence.

4

Ceasing to be
the Nearest Relative

This chapter considers the circumstances in which a patient's nearest relative will cease to be such.

Introduction

4.1 A patient's nearest relative need not remain so for ever. There are two circumstances in which a nearest relative might divest him- or herself, or be divested, of the role. They are:

1. where the nearest relative authorises someone else to perform his or her functions and

2. where an 'acting' nearest relative is appointed by the court, effectively displacing the original nearest relative.

Authorising someone else to be the nearest relative

4.2 The process by which a nearest relative might divest him- or herself of the role is set out, not in the Mental Health Act 1983 (MHA 1983), but in the regulations made under it.[1]

Giving an authority

4.3 A nearest relative may authorise someone else to perform his or her functions as nearest relative.[2] According to the MHA 1983 Code of Practice, the nearest relative might wish to do so where he or she 'would find it difficult to undertake

---

1   Mental Health (Hospital, Guardianship and Consent to Treatment) Regulations 1983, SI 1983 No 893 [Regulations]. See Appendix 2.

2   Regulations, reg 14(1).

the functions defined in the Act, or is reluctant for any reason to do this'. Furthermore, an Approved Social Worker (ASW) should consider proposing to a nearest relative that his or her functions be delegated to another person in an appropriate case.[3]

Example 51

Basheer has a sister, Zubaida, who is a patient within the meaning of the Mental Health Act 1983. Basheer, who has always respected his neighbour, Nathan, asks him to be Zubaida's nearest relative. Nathan is related neither to Basheer nor Zubaida, nor to their elder brother, Daleel. As the elder of Zubaida's brothers, Daleel would appear to be her nearest relative. Therefore, Basheer's preference is irrelevant and Nathan would need to be authorised by Daleel if he was to become Zubaida's nearest relative.

4.4 If the nearest relative gives such an authority, the person who receives it will exercise the relevant functions on behalf of the nearest relative.[4] It is the person to whom the authority is given who will be responsible for the performance of the nearest relative functions, and by giving the authority, the original nearest relative will divest him- or herself of responsibility in that regard.

4.5 Such an authority may be given at any time, whether or not the patient to whom it relates is, or is to be, detained or made subject to guardianship under MHA 1983.[5]

4.6 The nearest relative need not consult the patient before authorising someone else to perform his or her functions as nearest relative. Even if the patient is consulted by the nearest relative, the patient's view on the subject will carry no weight and may be disregarded.

4.7 There is nothing in MHA 1983 to require the nearest relative to obtain the consent of the person whom he or she authorises to perform his or her functions. Nevertheless, the system seems to assume that the person so authorised is willing to perform the functions of the nearest relative.

4.8 For any such authority to be valid, it must be given in writing.[6]

---

3   Department of Health and Welsh Office, *Mental Health Act 1983 Code of Practice*, 1999 [MHA 1983, *Code of Practice*], para. 2.17.
4   Regulations, reg 14(4).
5   Department of Health, *Mental Health Act 1983: Memorandum on Parts I to VI, VIII and X*, 1995, HMSO [MHA 1983 *Memorandum*], para. 62.
6   A specimen is set out in Appendix 3.

4.9 The person authorised to perform the functions of nearest relative need not be related to the patient.[7]

4.10 There are, however, some people who may not be authorised to perform the functions of the nearest relative.[8] They are:

- the patient him- or herself and

- anyone deemed not to be the nearest relative by virtue of section 26(5) of MHA 1983.[9]

4.11 The people whom section 26(5) deems not to be the nearest relative – who may not, therefore, be authorised to perform those functions – are:

- someone not 'ordinarily resident' in the United Kingdom, the Channel Islands or the Isle of Man, where the patient *is* so resident[10]

- a husband or wife of the patient, where the two are permanently separated (either by agreement or court order) or one has deserted the other[11]

- someone under 18 years of age who is neither a parent nor a spouse of the patient.[12]

Example 52

Norman is the nearest relative of his sister, Pamela, who, like him, lives in Norwich. Norman has grown weary of the role and wishes to assign it to someone else. He has narrowed the choice down to three people: Pamela's (and Norman's) brother, Bertrand, who lives in France; their other brother, Barry, who lives in London but is only 14 years of age; and Tommy, a good friend of Norman's, who lives in Brighton but is unknown to Pamela. Of these, it is only an authority given to Tommy that would divest Norman of the responsibility of being Pamela's nearest relative. Her two younger brothers are both ineligible: Bertrand because, while she is resident in the UK, he is not; and Barry because he is under 18. (If, rather than being unknown to Pamela, Tommy were her ex-husband, then he too would be prohibited from having the role of her nearest relative delegated to him. Norman would have to find someone else for that role, or else retain it himself. He could not, of course, authorise Pamela to perform it herself.)

---

7   MHA 1983 *Memorandum*, para. 62.
8   Regulations, reg 14(1).
9   See Appendix 1.
10   The concept of 'ordinary residence' is discussed in paras. **2.59–2.65**.
11   See paras. **2.21** and **2.22**.
12   MHA 1983, s 26(5).

4.12 If the nearest relative authorises someone else to perform his or her functions, he or she must forthwith give notice:

- to the person so authorised

- where the patient is detained in hospital under MHA 1983, to the managers of the hospital in which he or she is detained

- where the patient is subject to guardianship, to the local authority or private individual who is the patient's guardian.[13]

4.13 In the case of an *informal* patient, there is nothing to require a nearest relative who delegates his or her functions to give such notice to the hospital managers, nor is there anything to prohibit him or her from doing so.

4.14 Where the nearest relative authorises someone else to perform his or her functions, the authority will take effect when the other person receives it.[14]

Example 53

In the previous example, Norman decides to authorise Tommy to perform the nearest relative functions in respect of Pamela. He tells Tommy the news. Until he puts it in writing, however, the authority will not have been given and Norman will remain the nearest relative. In fact, that is the case unless and until the written authority is *received* by Tommy.

Example 54

Two days before Norman makes his decision, Pamela is admitted to hospital under section 2 of MHA 1983. Therefore, when Norman has put his authority in writing, he must give it not only to Tommy, but also to the managers of the hospital to which Pamela has been admitted.

Revoking an authority

4.15 Even if he or she has authorised someone else to perform his or her functions, a nearest relative will not forfeit the role entirely; for as long as he or she qualifies for the role, the nearest relative may revoke the authority.[15] Because the authorisation of a nearest relative must be in writing, it is likely that the revocation of the authorisation must also be in writing. (There is, however, no statutory requirement to this effect.)

---

13   Regulations, reg 14(2).
14   Regulations, reg 14(3).
15   Regulations, reg 14(1).

4.16 If the nearest relative revokes an authority that he or she gave to someone else, authorising the other person to perform the nearest relative functions, he or she must forthwith give notice to:

- the person so authorised
- where the patient is detained in hospital under MHA 1983, the managers of the hospital in which he or she is detained
- where the patient is subject to guardianship, the local authority or private individual who is the patient's guardian.[16]

4.17 If the authority related to an *informal* patient, the nearest relative would be well advised to notify the hospital managers that it has been revoked.

4.18 Where, having authorised another person to perform his or her functions, the nearest relative then revokes the authority, the revocation takes effect when the other person receives it.[17]

Expiry of an authority

4.19 Unless it is revoked, an authority given by the nearest relative will continue indefinitely. It will, however, come to an end:

- if the person to whom it was given dies
- if the person who gave it is displaced as nearest relative by the court or
- if the person who gave it dies or ceases for some other reason to be the patient's nearest relative.

4.20 This is to be contrasted with the position that obtains where a nearest relative is displaced by the court: then the person whom the court appoints acting nearest relative will remain in post, even if the original nearest relative dies or is demoted on the section 26 list.[18]

Example 55

In the last three examples above, Bertrand becomes ordinarily resident in the UK. Because he is also Pamela's brother, but older than Norman, he will become her nearest relative, and the authority Norman gave to Tommy will cease to have effect.

---

16   Regulations, reg 14(2).
17   Regulations, reg 14(3).
18   See paras. **4.71** and **4.72**.

Example 56

Bertrand dies shortly after his arrival in the UK, and being the next eldest, her brother, Norman becomes Pamela's nearest relative once again. As such, he is in a position to authorise someone else to exercise his functions, and could again choose Tommy in that regard. Tommy's previous authority has come to an end, however, so that if Tommy is indeed to exercise the nearest relative functions, a new authority will be required.

Example 57

Priyamkara is a patient under MHA 1983. His nearest relative, Nitesh, delegates his own powers as nearest relative to Donna. Nitesh dies and consequently, Donna ceases to be Priyamkara's nearest relative.

Example 58

In the previous example, if Donna had been appointed, not by Nitesh, but by the court, Nitesh's death would have had no impact upon her status: she would have remained Priyamkara's nearest relative.

Example 59

In the same example, if, Nitesh having delegated his powers to Donna, the court displaced Nitesh and appointed Alex as acting nearest relative, Donna's involvement would come to an end. In such circumstances, Alex would remain Priyamkara's nearest relative, notwithstanding Nitesh's death.

4.21   There is no fixed procedure whereby a person who no longer wishes to undertake the role of nearest relative might reject the authority given to him or her by the original nearest relative. He or she should, however, discuss his or her concerns with the original nearest relative, in the hope that that person might agree to revoke the authority.

4.22   The court has the power to direct that the functions of nearest relative be exercised by someone other than the person who would otherwise be entitled to exercise them.[19] That is assumed to be so whether the entitlement arises under section 29 of MHA 1983 or by virtue of an authority given by the person whom that section fixes with the role of nearest relative. That would mean, for example, that even where a person was authorised by the nearest relative to perform those functions in connection with a patient, he or she might have the power taken

---

19   MHA 1983, s 29(1).

away if he or she become incapable of acting as nearest relative by reason of mental disorder or other illness.[20] It is worth noting, however, that the court is only given an explicit power to displace the nearest relative, and that nothing in MHA 1983 explicitly confers that title upon a person who is merely *appointed* to the role. Indeed, in its only comment upon the relationship of the two individuals, the legislation says merely: 'A person for the time being authorised [to perform the functions of nearest relative] shall exercise [those functions] *on behalf of* the nearest relative.'[21]

Being displaced as nearest relative

4.23 The second circumstance in which the nearest relative might cease to be so is where an 'acting' nearest relative is appointed by the court, effectively displacing the original nearest relative.

4.24 The appointment of an acting nearest relative is covered in section 29 of MHA 1983.[22]

Application

4.25 An application for the appointment of an acting nearest relative must be made to the county court.[23] (Such applications are often referred to as 'displacement applications'.) At the moment, no such application may be made by the patient him- or herself.

4.26 A displacement application may be made by:

1. Any relative of the patient.[24] Relative means the same here as in s 26(1).[25] Therefore, the only relatives able to make application under section 29 are those that might have qualified as the patient's nearest relative in any event. A relative whose relationship with the patient is more distant than those set out in section 26(1) – for example, a cousin or stepchild of the patient – will not be able to apply under section 29 (unless he or she falls within paragraphs 2 or 3 below). The same is true of a concerned bystander.

2. Any other person with whom the patient is residing (or, if the patient is in hospital, with whom he or she was residing before admission to

20   MHA 1983, s 29(3)(b).
21   Regulations, reg 14(4) [emphasis added].
22   See also MHA 1983 *Memorandum*, paras. 107 and 108.
23   MHA 1983, s 29(1).
24   MHA 1983, s 29(2)(a).
25   See para. **2.9** *et seq.*

hospital).[26] There is no requirement that the applicant be someone with whom the patient *ordinarily* resides.[27] This would suggest that mere residence would be sufficient (and that no thought need be given to a patient's intentions, for example).

3. An ASW.[28] It is usually by an ASW that a displacement application is made.

The amended Act

The Government proposes to amend MHA 1983 to enable the patient him- or herself to seek the appointment of an acting nearest relative.[29]

Example 60

Sally is the nearest relative of her sister, Prunella, a MHA 1983 patient who lives alone. Barry is Sally's brother and Prunella's stepbrother. He believes Sally should not be Prunella's nearest relative. Even though he might have compelling reasons to do so, he cannot apply for Sally's displacement because his relationship with Prunella – that of stepbrother and stepsister – is not one of those set out in section 26, and therefore, he does not qualify as her 'relative' for the purposes of MHA 1983. It would seem that if there were to be an application, it would have to be made by an ASW. There might be a choice of applicants, however, if Prunella were residing with someone else or had a closer relative than Barry. (If the proposed amendment to the MHA 1983 is made, it is likely that Prunella herself will be able to apply for Sally to be displaced.)

4.27 MHA 1983 says only that in the relevant circumstances[30] a displacement application *may* be made; it does not say an application *must* be made.[31] Nevertheless, a person who failed to make an application in those circumstances might be called upon to explain his or her failure. That would be particularly so where the person concerned was an ASW.

4.28 As when performing his or her other functions under MHA 1983, an ASW who makes an application under section 29 will do so in a personal capacity. This means, for example, that he or she will not be bound to follow an instruction by

---

26   MHA 1983, s 29(2)(b).
27   The concept of 'ordinary residence' is discussed in paras. **2.59–2.65**.
28   MHA 1983, s 29(2)(c).
29   Department of Health and Home Office, *Mental Health Bill*, November 2006, HL Bill 1 54/2 [MHB 2006], cl 21.
30   See paras. **4.29–4.48**.
31   MHA 1983 *Memorandum*, para. 108.

the local authority employing him or her, either to make or not to make such an application. The local authority should, however:

- give an ASW proper assistance in such circumstances (and that will include proper legal assistance) and

- provide clear practical guidance on the relevant procedures, which it should discuss with the relevant court(s).[32]

Grounds

4.29 There are four grounds upon which an application may be made for the appointment of an acting nearest relative. They are set out in paragraphs 4.30 to 4.48 below.

THE FIRST GROUND

4.30 The first ground is that (a) the patient has no nearest relative within the meaning of MHA 1983, or (b) it is not reasonably practicable to ascertain whether he or she has a nearest relative, or who the nearest relative is.[33]

4.31 It might be appropriate to make an application on this ground where, for example, there is someone who does not qualify under section 26 but is nevertheless keen to perform the role of nearest relative.[34]

Example 61

Paulo lives on the moors, miles from anywhere, and was long thought never to associate, or even to have contact, with anyone else. He appears to have settled in Britain after the war and severed all links with his family in Italy. Recently, however, he has begun to receive visits from a local historian, Hector, with whom he has begun to discuss his life and experiences. It is likely that Paulo will have to be detained under MHA 1983, and desirable, therefore, that he should have a nearest relative. Because of their developing relationship, it might be appropriate to consider whether Hector should undertake that role, and if so, whether an application might be made to the court in that regard. (Any such application will, of course, have to be made by an ASW.)

---

32   MHA 1983 *Code of Practice*, para. 2.18.
33   MHA 1983, s 29(3)(a).
34   MHA 1983 *Memorandum*, para. 108.

THE SECOND GROUND

4.32 The second ground is that the person who is the patient's nearest relative by virtue of section 26 of MHA 1983 is incapable of acting as such by reason of mental disorder or other illness.[35]

4.33 If an order is to be made on this ground, it will have to be shown that the effect of the disorder or illness is to render the nearest relative *incapable* of fulfilling the functions the role carries. It will not be sufficient merely to show:

- that the nearest relative is suffering from mental disorder or another illness (without demonstrating its effect) or

- that the nearest relative has acted in an irresponsible or unwise manner (without establishing a disorder or illness, and a causal link between that and the nearest relative's irresponsibility or lack of wisdom).

4.34 It might not be necessary to apply to the court to displace a nearest relative who suffers from mental disorder. If the ASW concludes that because of the disorder, consultation with the nearest relative is 'not reasonably practicable', he or she may proceed with an application for the patient's admission under section 3 of MHA 1983 without having performed that consultation.[36] (However, and as discussed elsewhere,[37] it is only the duty to consult that will cease to apply in this circumstance. The other rights of the nearest relative will remain unaffected.)

Example 62

It is likely that Pattie will soon have to be detained in hospital under section 3 of MHA 1983. Pattie's nearest relative is her mother, Mavis, but she too is exhibiting signs of mental disorder. She claims that the television has spoken to her, although she seems to understand that this is probably a hallucination. As far as Pattie is concerned, Mavis is sure that she shouldn't be detained, but content that she receive treatment in hospital. It is unlikely that an application to displace Mavis would succeed: there is no suggestion that her mental disorder makes her incapable of being Pattie's nearest relative. (If, however, there are concerns that her capacity for the role will diminish in future, it might be suggested to Mavis that she delegate its performance to someone else.)

---

35   MHA 1983, s 29(3)(b).
36   MHA 1983, s 11(4).
37   See paras. **1.82** and **1.83**.

THE THIRD GROUND

4.35 The third ground is that the nearest relative unreasonably objects to the making of an application, either for admission for treatment or for guardianship, or that he or she is likely to do so.[38]

4.36 When deciding whether to make application under this ground, an ASW should consult his or her superiors and the doctors who, it is to be presumed, are willing to supply medical recommendations in support of any admission application.[39]

4.37 Whether or not it is *unreasonable* for the nearest relative to object to the patient's compulsory admission will be judged objectively.[40] In other words, a court will ask what a reasonable person would do in the circumstances that obtain (and it will be irrelevant that the nearest relative believed him- or herself to be acting reasonably). (This position may be contrasted with the latitude afforded to an ASW when he or she is called upon to determine a patient's nearest relative. The lawfulness of any such determination will be judged according to a *subjective* standard.[41])

4.38 The test the court will apply has been summarised as follows:

> [In] considering whether [he or] she is reasonable or unreasonable we must take into account the welfare of the [patient]. A reasonable [NR] surely gives great weight to what is better for the [patient]. [The nearest relative's] anguish of mind is quite understandable: but still it may be unreasonable for [him or] her to withhold consent.[42]

4.39 It is not the case, however, that there is one 'right' decision a nearest relative might make, and that all other decisions will therefore be 'wrong'. In each case, there will be a band of 'reasonable' responses, and provided his or her objection to admission falls within that band, a nearest relative need not fear being displaced.[43] So, for example, in a recent judgment it has been held that: '[I]t cannot possibly be outside that band of reasonable decisions for the [nearest relative] to agree with, and rely upon, a recent decision of a Mental Health Review Tribunal unless there has been a change in the circumstances leading to that decision'.[44] The case demonstrated, however, 'how difficult it is for the nearest relative to avoid being found unreasonable if his views differ from those of the hospital'.[45]

---

38   MHA 1983, s 29(3)(c).
39   MHA 1983 *Memorandum*, para. 108.
40   *W v L* [1974] QB 711, CA.
41   See paras. **5.59–5.62**.
42   *Re W (An Infant)* [1971] 2 All ER 59, *per* Lord Hailsham LC at 55, citing Lord Denning MR in *Re L (An Infant)* (1962) 106 Sol Jo 611 [interpolations are author's own].
43   *Re W (An Infant)* [1971] 2 All ER 49, *per* Lord Hailsham LC at 56.
44   *Smirek v Williams*, Court of Appeal, 7 April 2000 (unreported), *per* Hale LJ at [17].
45   *Ibid.*, at [15].

4.40 The use of an objective test in preference to a subjective one has been criticised, particularly because it implies that the nearest relative is simply a source of information for the professionals, and not an independent actor with a perspective of his or her own to lend to the case. Bartlett and Sandland suggest (2003):

> While the courts occasionally deny it, it is difficult to see that [section] 29 applications do not in the end collapse into a question of the court's view of the best interests of the patient, and the courts are loathe [*sic*] to take a view divergent from the patient's medical officers.[46]

4.41 Before adjudicating on the 'reasonableness' of any objection from the nearest relative, the court may wish to have evidence that compulsory admission to hospital is necessary. This is likely to come in the form of medical reports, or, more simply, of medical entries on the statutory admission forms. (The court should not, however, be influenced or distracted by any errors in the way those forms were completed.)[47]

Example 63

In the previous example, when the time comes, Mavis objects to Pattie being detained under section 3 of MHA 1983. She says that neither the ASW nor the doctors truly understand Pattie's condition, and that they are far too eager to resort to detention. Though it will be possible to apply for Mavis to be displaced as nearest relative, it might be difficult to show on objective grounds that her objection to detention is unreasonable. The position would probably be different if she had given as the reason for her objection the suspicion that the world's doctors have combined forces to outwit her. (This suspicion might also support displacement on the ground that Mavis is *incapable* of performing the role of nearest relative.)

THE FOURTH GROUND

4.42 The fourth ground is that the nearest relative has exercised – or is likely to exercise – the power to discharge the patient from hospital or guardianship, and that such was (or would be) without due regard to the welfare of the patient or the interests of the public.[48]

4.43 Where a nearest relative has exercised, or is likely to exercise, the discharge power in such a way, 'the staff of the hospital concerned should consult the local

---

46   See, for example, Bartlett and Sandland 2003, pp.206–207.
47   *B (A) v B (L) (Mental Health Patient)* [1980] 1 WLR 116, CA.
48   MHA 1983, s 29(3)(d).

social services authority, and if it is decided to apply to a county court, the hospital should provide any necessary evidence to support the application'.[49]

4.44 Where the nearest relative has already exercised the power of discharge, a displacement application should only be made if it is expected that the patient will be admitted to hospital again within three months.[50]

4.45 Whether or not, in exercising the power of discharge, a nearest relative had *due regard* to the patient's welfare or the public interest will, again, be judged objectively.[51] In other words, a court will ask what a reasonable person would do in the circumstances that obtain (and it will be irrelevant that the nearest relative believed him- or herself to have had due regard to the relevant factors).

4.46 It is a moot point whether, *before* the nearest relative has exercised the discharge power, it can ever be concluded that if he or she were to do so it would be 'without due regard'. The court surely cannot know in advance the factors to which the nearest relative will have regard when the time comes.

Example 64

In the previous two examples, Mavis finally withdraws her objection, with the result that the displacement proceedings come to an end. Once Pattie is detained, however, Mavis purports to discharge her under section 23(2)(a) of MHA 1983. She says that in the five days that Pattie has been in hospital, she has received no medication, has not seen a doctor and has been allowed to abscond on no less than four occasions. She says she can provide better – and safer – care for Pattie at home. Though it will be possible to apply for Mavis to be displaced as nearest relative, it might be difficult to show on objective grounds that she used her discharge power without due regard to Pattie's welfare or the interests of the public. (This will be especially so if, a barring certificate having been issued by Pattie's Responsible Medical Officer, a Mental Health Review Tribunal subsequently decided that Pattie was not 'dangerous' and that she should therefore be discharged from detention.) The position would probably be different if Mavis had given as her reason for discharging Pattie the belief that the world's doctors were against her. (Again, that belief might also support displacement on the ground that Mavis is *incapable* of performing the role of nearest relative.)

---

49   MHA 1983 *Memorandum*, para. 110.
50   *Ibid.*
51   *Surrey County Council Social Services Department v McMurray*, Court of Appeal, 11 November 1994 (unreported).

4.47 At present, there are no other grounds upon which a displacement application might be made.

The amended Act

Among the proposed amendments to MHA 1983 is one that would add a further ground for displacement: that the nearest relative of the patient is 'not a suitable person to act as such'.[52]

4.48 If the displacement application is to succeed, the ground(s) upon which it is based must exist, not only at the time of application, but also at the time of the final hearing.[53] This means, for example, that a nearest relative who does not object to the making of an admission application may not be displaced merely because he or she previously *did* object at the time the application was made and was believed to have done so unreasonably.

Procedure

4.49 The procedure for dealing with an application under section 29 of MHA 1983 is set out in Order 49, rule 12 of the County Court Rules (which now appears in Schedule 2 to the Civil Procedure Rules 1998[54]).

4.50 This means, for example, that:

- such an application should be made to the county court for the district in which the patient resides[55]

- the nearest relative must be made a party to the application, unless: (a) the application has been made under section 29(3)(a) on the ground either that the patient has no nearest relative, or that it is not reasonably practicable to ascertain who the nearest relative is; or (b) the court orders that the nearest relative need not be made a party[56]

- the court may order that someone else be made a party to the application.[57] A patient may (and should) be given an opportunity to participate in the proceedings.[58]

---

52   MHB 2006, cl 21(5)(b).
53   *Brenda Lewis v Mark Gibson* [2005] EWCA Civ 587, at [38].
54   SI 1998 No.132.
55   County Court Rules ['CCR'] Order 49, Rule 12(2).
56   CCR Order 49, Rule 12(3)(a).
57   CCR Order 49, Rule 12(3)(b).
58   *Brenda Lewis v Mark Gibson* [2005] EWCA Civ 587, *per* Thorpe LJ at [40] and Wall LJ at [44]-[46].

4.51 Where a section 29 application is made because the nearest relative is incapable of acting as such by reason of mental disorder, it is likely that a 'litigation friend' will have to be appointed for him or her.[59] This will certainly be so where the nearest relative's mental disorder comes within the meaning of MHA 1983 and renders him or her incapable of managing and administering his or her own property and affairs.[60] In those circumstances, the requirements of Part 21 of the Civil Procedure Rules will have to be fulfilled.[61] It is likely that the Official Solicitor will agree to act as the litigation friend of a nearest relative in these circumstances, and possible that he or she will appoint local agents to act on the latter's behalf at any court hearing.

4.52 When it is received by the court, a section 29 application will be dealt with by a circuit judge. (In other words, it cannot be dealt with by a mere district judge.)[62]

4.53 Displacement applications 'have to be dealt with quickly'.[63] However, there is at least one case in which such an application was not heard for a year,[64] and another in which proceedings were only finally disposed of after two years.[65] Until – and unless – the court appoints an acting nearest relative, the original nearest relative will continue to enjoy the powers granted by MHA 1983, even though a displacement application has been made and is waiting to be heard. (However, the court may make a displacement order on an *ex parte* or an interim basis.[66])

4.54 Unless the court orders otherwise, a displacement application will be heard in private.[67]

4.55 The patient may be interviewed by the judge or, at the judge's direction, by a district judge. Any such interview may, but need not, (a) take place in the presence of the other parties, or (b) be held at court.[68]

4.56 When hearing a displacement application, the court may accept as evidence of the facts it contains any report made by a medical practitioner.[69]

---

59   Civil Procedure Rules 1998 ['CPR'], 21.2(1).
60   CPR 21.1(2)(b).
61   Available at www.dca.gov.uk/civil/procrules_fin/contents/parts/part21.htm See also: CPR, *Practice Direction 21 – Children and patients* – www.dca.gov.uk/civil/procrules_fin/contents/practice_directions/pd_part21.htm
62   CPR, *Practice Direction – Allocation of cases to levels of judiciary*, para. 11.1(a)(vii) – www.dca.gov.uk/civil/procrules_fin/contents/practice_directions/pd_part2b.htm
63   *R (Stevens) v Plymouth City Council* [2002] EWCA Civ 388, *per* Hale LJ at [39].
64   *Derbyshire County Council v Maude* [1999] EWCA Civ 1760, *per* Sedley LJ.
65   *R (MH) v Secretary of State for Health* [2005] UKHL 60.
66   See paras. **4.61–4.64**.
67   CCR Order 49, Rule 12(5).
68   CCR Order 49, Rule 12(6).
69   CCR Order 49, Rule 12(4).

4.57 The court may also accept as evidence of the facts it contains any report made in the course of his or her official duties by:

- a probation officer[70]

- an officer of a local authority

- an officer of a voluntary organisation exercising statutory functions on behalf of a local authority[71] or

- an officer of a hospital authority.[72]

4.58 Where, in the course of displacement proceedings, a court considers such a report, the nearest relative 'shall be told the substance of any part of the report bearing on his [or her] fitness or conduct which the judge considers to be material for the fair determination of the application'.[73] The patient may challenge such a report, and will be able to introduce evidence of his or her own in order to do so.

DISCLOSURE[74]

4.59 Where displacement proceedings are begun because a patient is to be brought under MHA 1983, or because the nearest relative has used his or her power of discharge, the court should be given the basic documents: the admission application form and the medical recommendations (and any renewal reports). Although it has been suggested that it would be sufficient for disclosure of any such documents to be given to the nearest relative's legal representative,[75] the Court of Appeal has more recently held that they should also be disclosed to the nearest relative personally (and to the other parties).[76] The only exception to this rule would be where there were competing factors, such as national security or risk to a child, which might outweigh it.

4.60 In fact, the Court of Appeal has gone further, suggesting that disclosure should be governed by the same considerations in displacement proceedings as in Mental Health Review Tribunal (MHRT) proceedings.[77] This would mean that:

- a nearest relative would be entitled to see every relevant document received by the court unless disclosure would adversely affect the health or welfare of the patient or someone else;[78] but

---

70   CCR Order 49, Rule 12(4)(a).
71   CCR Order 49, Rule 12(4)(b).
72   CCR Order 49, Rule 12(4)(c).
73   CCR Order 49, Rule 12(4).
74   See also para. **5.77** *et seq.*
75   *B (A) v B (L) (Mental Health Patient)* [1980] 1 WLR 116.
76   *R (Stevens) v Plymouth City Council and another* [2002] EWCA Civ 388, *per* Hale LJ at [36] and [41]. See also: *Re D (Adoption Reports: Confidentiality)* [1996] AC 593, *per* Lord Mustill at p.615.
77   *R (Stevens) v Plymouth City Council and another* [2002] EWCA Civ 388, *per* Hale LJ at [38].
78   Mental Health Review Tribunal Rules 1983 [MHRT Rules], rr 6(4) and 12(2). See para. **7.68.**

- even if a document were withheld from a nearest relative on such grounds, it would still have to be disclosed to any legal representative he or she chose to instruct.[79]

HEARINGS *ex parte*

4.61 The county court may hear a section 29 application on an *ex parte* basis; in other words, in the absence of one or more of the parties.[80] (In one case, a nearest relative was given two hours' notice of a 'displacement' hearing and not served with any papers.[81]) The 'basic requirements of fairness in legal proceedings' dictate that if the circumstances so permit, the nearest relative, as well as the patient or his or her legal representative, must be informed of a displacement hearing before it takes place.[82] Furthermore, it is good practice for a judge hearing an *ex parte* displacement application to inquire whether it was practicable for an absent party to be notified of the hearing, and his or her failure to do so might be a basis for an appeal against any interim displacement order. However, the failure either to give notice of an *ex parte* hearing or to enquire why no such notice was given will not deprive the court of its power to displace the nearest relative.[83]

4.62 If an order is made against him or her without notice, a nearest relative may apply for it to be set aside or varied on that ground alone.[84]

INTERIM ORDERS

4.63 Whether or not the relevant hearing is held *ex parte*, a court may make an interim order under section 29, appointing an acting nearest relative until the application can be heard in full.[85]

4.64 Where the court makes such an interim order, it is the case both (a) that an admission application may be made by an ASW on the basis of his or her consultation with the *interim* acting nearest relative, and (b) that the managers to whom that application is addressed may lawfully accept it.[86] However, where the application was made – and the interim order granted – because the nearest relative unreasonably objected to the making of an application:

---

79   MHRT Rules, r 12(3). See para. **7.71**.
80   CPR 23.8. See also: CPR, *Practice Direction 23*, para. 3.
81   *R v Uxbridge County Court, ex parte Binns* [2000] MHLR 179.
82   *R (Adrian Holloway) v Oxfordshire County Council, Oxford County Court and Oxfordshire and Buckinghamshire Mental Health Partnership NHS Trust* [2007] EWHC 776 (Admin), *per* Beatson J at [33].
83   *Ibid.*, at [43] and [49].
84   CPR 23.10(1).
85   County Court Act 1984, s 38. See Appendix 2.
86   *R v Central London County Court, ex parte London* [1999] 3 All ER 991, CA.

- 'it is preferable' that the application be heard in full before an admission application is made, 'unless there are cogent reasons to the contrary'[87] and

- where a patient is detained following an interim order, it has been suggested that he or she will have to be released if the court declines to make a final order displacing the nearest relative.[88]

Order

4.65 Having heard an application under section 29, the judge will have the discretion to decide whether or not to make an order, and he or she may decline to do so, even if one or more of the grounds has been established.[89]

4.66 The county court may order that the functions of the nearest relative in respect of a patient[90] be exercisable by another, named person.[91] (This is the only part the court may play. Having made, or declined to make, such an order, the court will have no continuing role in the care and treatment of the patient under MHA 1983.)

APPLICATION BY AN APPROVED SOCIAL WORKER

4.67 If the application was made by an ASW, the court may appoint as acting nearest relative, not him or her, but (a) the relevant local social services authority or (b) someone named in the application.[92] Each social services authority should ensure that its scheme of delegation allows for the role of acting nearest relative, conferred upon it in this way, to be performed by the director of social services. (Separate arrangements will have to be made if the director is, in turn, to nominate someone else to exercise the powers delegated to him or her in this way.)

APPLICATION BY SOMEONE ELSE

4.68 If the application was made by someone other than an ASW, the person whom the court names as acting nearest relative will be (a) the applicant or (b) someone named in the application.[93]

---

87   *Ibid., per* Stuart-Smith L.J. at para. 24.
88   *Ibid., per* Stuart-Smith L.J. at para. 22.
89   *Barnet LBC v Robin* [1998] EWCA Civ 1630. As to the relevant grounds, see paras. **4.29–4.46**.
90   See Chapter 5.
91   MHA 1983, s 29(1).
92   MHA 1983 s 29(1) and (2).
93   MHA 1983, s 29(1).

4.69 The court does not have *carte blanche* with regard to an acting nearest relative: it may not name someone who was neither the applicant nor named in the application.[94]

The amended Act

It seems that the amended MHA 1983 will give a court the power to appoint as acting nearest relative not only the person who made, or was named in, the relevant application, but, in the alternative, anyone else who, in its opinion, is a suitable person to act as such.[95]

4.70 Before naming someone as nearest relative, the court will have to be satisfied (a) that he or she is a proper person to act as nearest relative and (b) that he or she is willing to do so.[96] (It would be prudent, to say the least, for an applicant to ensure that the relevant person is willing to act as nearest relative, and to take steps in that regard before the application is made.)

Example 65

Having heard an application made in respect of a patient, Prakash, the court decides that his nearest relative should be displaced. The application was made by an ASW, Alfie, but the court must overlook him. It may appoint as acting nearest relative the relevant local social services authority or someone whom Alfie named in his application. If the application had been made not by Alfie, but by Prakash's sister, Sunita, the court might appoint as acting nearest relative Sunita, or anyone she had named. In neither case may the court pluck a name out of thin air.

Effect of order

4.71 Where the county court makes an order directing that the functions of a patient's nearest relative be exercisable by a named person, that person will be the patient's nearest relative and will be entitled to exercise those functions as long as the order continues in force. This is so, even where, by making its order, the court effectively displaced the original nearest relative and that person no longer has priority according to the statutory list (because, for example, he or she has died).[97]

---

94   *Ibid.*
95   MHB 2006, cl 21(3).
96   MHA 1983, s 29(1).
97   MHA 1983, s 29(6).

4.72 This is to be contrasted with the position that obtains where a person becomes nearest relative not as the result of a court order, but by virtue of an authority granted by the original nearest relative. In those circumstances, the person authorised will forfeit his or her role if the original nearest relative dies or loses priority on the statutory list.[98]

4.73 The displaced nearest relative does not lose all of his or her powers. If, following the appointment of an acting nearest relative, the patient subsequently becomes liable to be detained or subject to guardianship, the displaced nearest relative may apply to the MHRT for the patient's case to be reviewed. One such application may be made within 12 months of the displacement order, and a further such application within each succeeding 12-month period.[99] (The acting nearest relative will also have the right to apply to the MHRT.[100])

4.74 In addition, the displaced nearest relative will continue to have a 'legitimate interest' in the welfare of the patient, which 'should always be paid proper respect by the authorities in making decisions about and arrangements for [the patient's] care'.[101] (It is likely that the interest of a relative will not be 'legitimate' where the circumstances are such that, following the case of *E v Bristol City Council*, it would be considered 'impracticable' to consult him or her about a patient's detention under section 3 of MHA 1983.[102])

Example 66

In the last example, the nearest relative whom the court displaced was Prakash's mother, Meera. Though displaced, Meera will not forfeit all her rights: she will still be entitled to make one application to the MHRT in respect of Prakash per year, and to be taken into consideration when the authorities make any decisions about his care.

4.75 Where a local social services authority is appointed acting nearest relative, it will have additional responsibilities towards the patient if he or she is admitted to hospital or to a care home.[103] Those responsibilities will apply whether the treatment the patient is to receive is for a mental disorder or for a physical disorder. In particular, the authority must:

---

98   See paras. **4.19** and **4.20**.
99   MHA 1983, ss 29(6) and 66(1)(h) and (2)(g).
100   MHA 1983, ss 29(6) and 66(1). See para. **7.39**.
101   *Surrey County Council Social Services Department v McMurray*, November 11 1995, CA, *per* Hale J.
102   *R (E) v Bristol City Council* [2005] EWHC 74 (Admin). See paras. **1.80–1.84**.
103   MHA 1983, s 116.

- arrange for the patient to be visited and

- take such other steps in relation to the patient was would be expected to be taken by his or her parents.

Duration of order

4.76 When making an order under section 29, the court may specify the period for which it is to continue in force,[104] but only if the order was made because:

- the patient has no nearest relative within the meaning of MHA 1983, or it is not reasonably practicable to ascertain whether he has a nearest relative or who the nearest relative is[105] or

- the person who is the patient's nearest relative by virtue of section 26 of MHA 1983 is incapable of acting as such by reason of mental disorder or other illness.[106]

The amended Act

If MHA 1983 is amended as the Government has proposed, the court will also be able to specify the duration of any displacement order made at the patient's request.[107]

4.77 This means that the court may not specify the duration of a displacement order made because the nearest relative:

- unreasonably objected – or was likely so to object – to the making of an application[108] or

- exercised – or was likely to exercise – the discharge power without due regard to the welfare of the patient or the interests of the public.[109]

4.78 If it has the power to do so, the court might choose to specify the duration of a displacement order where, for example, the patient has children who could become his or her nearest relative, but none of them is yet 18 years of age. The court could appoint an acting nearest relative until the eldest child attains his or her majority.[110]

---

104   MHA 1983, s 29(5).
105   MHA 1983, s 29(3)(a). See paras. **4.30** and **4.31**.
106   MHA 1983, s 29(3)(b). See paras. **4.32–4.34**.
107   MHB 2006, cl 21(6).
108   MHA 1983, s 29(3)(c).
109   MHA 1983, s 29(3)(d).
110   MHA 1983 *Memorandum*, para. 108.

4.79 If the court specifies the period for which a displacement order is to remain in force,[111] the order will remain in force for that period (unless it is discharged or varied within that period[112]).[113]

4.80 If the court did not – or *could* not – specify the period during which it was to remain in force, a displacement order will come to an end:

- when the patient ceases to be detained or subject to guardianship, if he was so when the order was made or became so within three months thereafter[114] or

- once three months have elapsed since the date of the displacement order, if he wasn't detained or subject to guardianship at the time and hasn't become so subsequently.[115]

The amended Act

Under the amendments proposed by the Government, it would only be a displacement order granted because of (a) an unreasonable objection by the nearest relative or (b) his or her use of the discharge power without due regard that would come to an end in this way. An order granted because a patient had no nearest relative, or because the nearest relative could not be ascertained or was incapable of acting as such, would terminate at the end of the period specified by the court or, where no period was specified, upon application. It might, therefore, prove to be of indefinite duration.[116]

4.81 Discharge is the only event in a patient's detention that might bring an end to an order displacing the nearest relative; an order transferring the patient to another hospital, or from hospital to guardianship (or *vice versa*) will not have that effect.[117]

4.82 Whether or not the court specifies – or is *able* to specify – for how long a displacement order is to remain in force, the order might still be discharged or varied by the court in the circumstances set out in MHA 1983, section 30.[118]

---

111   See paras. **4.76–4.79**.
112   MHA 1983, s 30(1)–(3). See paras. **4.83–4.91**.
113   MHA 1983, s 30(4).
114   MHA 1983, s 30(4)(a).
115   MHA 1983, s 30(4)(b).
116   MHB 2006, cl 22(7).
117   MHA 1983 *Memorandum*, para. 109.
118   See paras. **4.80–4.91**.

Example 67

Phoebe is detained under section 3 of MHA 1983, and her nearest relative is her brother, Ben. The court displaces Ben because it considers him incapable of acting as nearest relative by reason of his own mental disorder, and it specifies that the displacement order shall continue for three months – that is, until Phoebe's daughter, Diane, attains her majority. Ben will be displaced for the next three months, unless, in the interim, the order is varied or discharged by the court.

Example 68

If Ben were displaced, not by reason of his incapacity, but because, for example, he had exercised his power to discharge Phoebe without due regard to her welfare, the court would not have had the power to specify the duration of the displacement order and, unless it was varied or discharged by the court in the interim, the order would end only when Phoebe was eventually discharged from detention.

The discharge or variation of a displacement order

4.83 A displacement order may be (a) varied or (b) discharged upon application to the court.[119]

DISCHARGE

4.84 An application to discharge a displacement order may be made by the acting nearest relative.[120]

4.85 An application to discharge a displacement order may be made by the nearest relative, if:

- the displacement order was made *either* because the patient had no nearest relative within the meaning of MHA 1983, *or* because it was not reasonably practicable to ascertain whether he had a nearest relative or who the nearest relative was

- the displacement order was made because the nearest relative was incapable of acting as such by reason of mental disorder or other illness or

---

119   MHA 1983, s 30.
120   MHA 1983, s 30(1)(a).

- the nearest relative has now ceased to be such (for example, because the patient has now married and the spouse has thereby become the nearest relative).[121]

4.86 This means that the nearest relative cannot apply to discharge a displacement order made because: he or she (a) unreasonably objected – or was likely so to object – to the making of an application; or (b) exercised – or was likely to exercise – the discharge power without due regard to the welfare of the patient or the interests of the public.[122] Only the *acting* nearest relative may apply for discharge or variation of a displacement order made on one of those grounds.

The amended Act

Where a court, using the power granted under an amendment to MHA 1983, makes an order displacing a nearest relative because he or she is not a suitable person to act as such, the nearest relative so displaced will only be able to apply for the discharge of that order with the leave of the court.[123]

VARIATION

4.87 An application to vary a displacement order may be made (a) by the acting nearest relative or (b) by an ASW.[124] The only permitted result of such an application would be to replace the acting nearest relative with either a local social services authority or someone the court considered a proper person for the role.[125] This means, for example, that an order may not be varied by substituting an individual for a local authority nearest relative, or by replacing one local authority with another. (In fact, of course, the local authority could simply *delegate* its nearest relative functions to another person or another authority.[126])

4.88 Where the acting nearest relative dies:

- an application either to discharge or to vary the displacement order may be made by any relative of the patient[127] and

- until – and unless – the order is discharged or varied, no one will be able to exercise the nearest relative functions with regard to the patient.[128]

---

121   MHA 1983, s 30(1)(b).
122   MHA 1983, s 29(3)(d).
123   MHB 2006, cl 22(3).
124   MHA 1983, s 30(2).
125   *Ibid.*
126   See paras. **4.2–4.22**.
127   MHA 1983, s 30(3)(a).
128   MHA 1983, s 30(3)(b).

4.89 Where a displacement order is discharged or varied subsequently, that will not affect the validity of anything done in pursuance of it.[129]

Summary

- An acting nearest relative may apply for either discharge or variation of a displacement order.
- A displaced nearest relative may apply for discharge, but not where he or she was displaced of grounds of having acted (a) unreasonably or (b) without due regard. He or she may not apply for variation.
- An ASW may apply for variation of a displacement order, but not for its discharge.
- Any relative of the patient may apply to vary or discharge a displacement order, but only where the acting nearest relative has died.

4.90 An application to vary or discharge an order made under section 29 of MHA 1983 shall be made to the court that made the order.[130]

4.91 Unless the court orders otherwise, a displacement application will be heard in private.[131]

Miscellaneous

4.92 If, at the time an application is made for an acting nearest relative to be appointed with regard to a patient, the latter is detained under section 2 of MHA 1983, then the period of his or her detention might not come to an end after 28 days. It will last until:

- the application has been finally disposed of, if no such appointment is made[132] or
- if an order *is* made, for a further seven days after the application has been finally disposed of.[133]

4.93 An application under section 29 will have been made once a claim form has been issued by the court.[134]

---

129   MHA 1983, s 30(5).
130   CCR Order 49, Rule 12(2).
131   CCR Order 49, Rule 12(5).
132   MHA 1983, s 29(4)(a).
133   MHA 1983, s 29(4)(b).
134   CPR 7.2(1).

4.94 An application under section 29 of MHA 1983 will be regarded as having been 'finally disposed of':

- where no appeal has been made against the court's decision (whether or not it was to appoint an acting nearest relative) and the time for making it has expired or

- where an appeal has been made and either heard or withdrawn.[135]

4.95 However, there is at least one case in which a displacement application was not heard for a year,[136] and another in which proceedings were only finally disposed of after two years.[137]

135   MHA 1983, s 29(4).
136   *Derbyshire County Council v Maude* [1999] EWCA Civ 1760, *per* Sedley LJ.
137   *R (MH) v Secretary of State for Health* [2005] UKHL 60.

5

Admission
and the Nearest Relative

This chapter considers the powers of the nearest relative where a patient is – or is to be – admitted to hospital under the Mental Health Act 1983.

Introduction

5.1 The nearest relative of a patient detained under the Mental Health Act 1983 (MHA 1983) has a number of significant powers. These:

1. arise before a patient's admission

2. apply to, and continue during, admission

3. relate to consultation and the providing of information and

4. enable the nearest relative to discharge a patient from detention, or at least to apply to a Mental Health Review Tribunal (MHRT) to the same end.[1]

5.2 This chapter considers each of these circumstances. It is worth noting, however, that where the patient is a both a child and a ward of court, these powers may only be exercised with the permission of the court.[2]

5.3 Aside from his or her rights under MHA 1983, a nearest relative who gives a patient substantial and regular care might, like a non-nearest relative carer, be entitled to an annual assessment of his or her own needs,[3] and even to specific carer services.[4] These entitlements do not arise from the nearest relative's status under the Act, however, and they are therefore beyond the scope of this book.[5]

---

1   For discussion of this last right, see para. **7.36** *et seq.*
2   MHA 1983, s 33(2).
3   Carers (Recognition and Services) Act 1995, s 1; Carers and Disabled Children's Act 2000, s 1. See also: Department of Health 1999a, Standard 6; Department of Health 1999b.
4   Carers and Disabled Children's Act 2000, s 2.
5   But see, for example: Clements 2004, especially Chapter 11; Mandelstam 2005, Chapter 12; Brown 2006, pp.56–58.

Before admission

5.4 As we shall see, it is possible for either an Approved Social Worker (ASW) or the nearest relative to make application for a patient's admission to hospital or reception into guardianship.[6]

The best applicant

5.5 If possible, an admission application should be made by an ASW. The MHA 1983 Memorandum acknowledges that the nearest relative 'may often prefer that the [ASW] should sign an application' for admission;[7] and the MHA 1983 Code of Practice says:

> The ASW is usually the right applicant, bearing in mind professional training, knowledge of the legislation and of local resources, together with the potential adverse effect that an application by the nearest relative might have on the latter's relationship with the patient.[8]

5.6 A doctor who undertakes an assessment under MHA 1983 should therefore advise the nearest relative that where there is to be an admission application in respect of the patient, it is preferable that it be made by an ASW.[9] The doctor should inform the nearest relative of his or her rights to require an assessment,[10] and should not advise him or her to make an application simply to avoid the need for assessment by an ASW.[11]

5.7 In fact, where detention is in prospect, it should always be possible for a patient to be assessed by an ASW. The Code of Practice says:

> A nearest relative should not be put in the position of having to make an application for admission under the Act because it is not possible for an ASW to attend for assessment. Subject to resources, local authorities should provide a 24-hour ASW service to ensure that this does not happen.[12]

5.8 Local authorities should have explicit policies on how to respond to repeated requests for assessment where the condition of the patient has not changed significantly.[13]

---

6   See paras. **5.30–5.38** and **5.39–5.43**.
7   Department of Health, *Mental Health Act 1983: Memorandum on Parts I to VI, VIII and X*, 1995, HMSO [MHA 1983 *Memorandum*], para. 32.
8   Department of Health and Welsh Office, *Mental Health Act 1983 Code of Practice*, 1999 [MHA 1983 *Code of Practice*], para. 2.35.
9   *Ibid.*
10   Under MHA 1983, s 13(4). MHA 1983 *Code of Practice*, para. 2.35. See paras. **5.9–5.16**.
11   MHA 1983 *Code of Practice*, para. 2.36.
12   *Ibid.*, para. 2.37.
13   *Ibid.*, para. 2.38.

Requiring that a patient's case be taken into consideration

5.9 Under section 13(4) of MHA 1983, a nearest relative may require the relevant local social services authority to direct an ASW to take a patient's case into consideration with a view to making an application for the patient to be admitted to hospital. By resorting to this power, a nearest relative would be insisting, in essence, that the patient be assessed for possible detention.

5.10 Where such a requirement is made by the nearest relative:

- the local authority will be responsible for receiving it and, if it is properly made, for directing an ASW to take the patient's case into consideration

- it would seem that the local authority has no discretion in the matter: if the requirement is properly made, the authority will have to issue a direction to an ASW[14]

- the ASW will be responsible for the manner in which, in response to such a direction, he or she takes the patient's case into consideration.

5.11 There is nothing to say that a nearest relative must put any such requirement in writing, and it is likely that it can be purely verbal in nature. The requirement might not be made in so many words, however, and ASWs and local authorities should pay particular attention to suggestions by a nearest relative to the effect that something 'ought to be done', or that a patient 'should be in hospital'.[15]

5.12 In any discussions between them, the ASW should ensure that the nearest relative is aware of this power.

5.13 It is the local authority alone that may issue a direction and thereby initiate the section 13(4) process. Therefore, if a nearest relative directs his or her requirement to the ASW, the ASW should pass it to the local authority and await the making of a direction by that body.

5.14 It is possible that a requirement of the kind made possible by section 13(4) will be communicated through an intermediary. The Code of Practice says that local authorities should give guidance to ASWs as to whether a request from a nearest relative may be accepted via a GP or other professional. (Such a request should be accepted, provided the nearest relative intends that it be passed on to the local authority.)[16]

---

14   But cf. paras. **5.15** and **5.16**.
15   See: Jones 2006, paras. 1–150.
16   MHA 1983 *Code of Practice*, para. 2.38.

5.15 The obligation of a local authority under section 13(4) exists only in relation to 'a patient'. The definition of this word in MHA 1983 is: 'a person suffering or appearing to be suffering from mental disorder'.[17] This means that even though a nearest relative might require it to make a direction, the local authority need not do so if it concludes that the patient is (a) neither suffering nor appearing to be suffering from mental disorder or (b) not residing within its area. Any such conclusion should be communicated to the nearest relative in writing, and because it might be susceptible to legal challenge, it should be based upon compelling, current grounds.

5.16 Likewise, there is no power for the nearest relative to require that a direction be given to an ASW where the objective is not a patient's admission to hospital, but his or her reception into guardianship.

Taking a patient's case into consideration

5.17 If, in response to a requirement made by the nearest relative under section 13(4) of MHA 1983, the local authority directs an ASW take a patient's case into consideration, he or she must act as soon as practicable.[18]

5.18 The only obligation in section 13(4) is placed upon the local authority that is required to act by the nearest relative. Though the authority might employ the ASW, the latter is in law an independent actor and may decide autonomously whether to take the patient's case into consideration. The ASW might decline to do so if, for example he or she concludes that the patient is (a) neither suffering nor appearing to be suffering from mental disorder, or (b) not residing within the area of the relevant local authority. Any such conclusion should be communicated to the nearest relative in writing, and because it might be susceptible to legal challenge, it should be based upon compelling, current grounds.

5.19 There is nothing in MHA 1983 (or the Code of Practice) to say what the process of taking a patient's case into consideration will involve. It is likely that it is less intensive than the process an ASW is required to complete before making an application for admission to hospital, when it is essential, of course, that he or she 'interview the patient in a suitable manner'.[19]

5.20 The nature and extent of the process will vary according to the circumstances, and in particular, according to what is known about the patient. It might, however, be influenced by such things as:

---

17   MHA 1983, s 145(1).
18   MHA 1983, s 13(4).
19   MHA 1983, s 13(2).

- how recently an ASW last took the patient's case into consideration
- whether the patient is currently receiving services for a mental disorder (either as an outpatient or as an inpatient)
- what, in general, is known about the patient, and in particular, about his or her social and family circumstances
- what other professionals – such as the patient's GP – have to say about the patient
- what is known about the nearest relative. (As Richard Jones puts it, 'It could be that the nearest relative is the mentally disordered member of the 'patient's family'.[20])

5.21 The ASW taking the patient's case into consideration will do so 'with a view to making an application for his admission to hospital'.[21] This is likely to be less exacting than the exercise that will precede an admission application, in which an ASW must

> satisfy himself that detention in a hospital is in all the circumstances of the case the most appropriate way of providing the care and medical treatment of which the patient stands in need.[22]

5.22 Both the process of taking a patient's case into consideration and its result should be recorded in writing.

5.23 Having received a direction to that effect, the ASW will be personally liable for the way a patient's case is taken into consideration – or, if appropriate, for the decision not to take the case into consideration.

Deciding not to apply for admission

5.24 Even though the ASW may take a patient's case into consideration, there is nothing to require him or her subsequently to make an application for a patient's admission to hospital or to guardianship.[23]

5.25 If the ASW decides not to make an application, that is not, however, the end of his or her responsibilities. The ASW must also:

- reflect on any needs that he or she has assessed the patient to have, and on how those needs are to be met

20   Jones 2006, para. 1–150.
21   MHA 1983, s 13(5).
22   MHA 1983, s 13(2).
23   MHA 1983, s 13(5).

- ensure that the nearest relative has a clear understanding of any alternative arrangements and
- record those arrangements in writing.[24]

5.26 The ASW must also discuss the reasons for his or her decision with the nearest relative.[25] This is so whether or not assessment by the ASW was precipitated by a formal requirement by the nearest relative (and a direction by the local authority).

5.27 If, however, the involvement of the ASW was brought about by the nearest relative under section 13(4), the ASW must confirm his or her reasons in writing.[26] (Those reasons might include the fact that the ASW has concluded that the patient is not, in truth, a 'patient' within the meaning of MHA 1983.)

5.28 When drafting any reasons, the ASW should take care not to breach the patient's confidentiality in a way that might infringe the common law or the Human Rights Act 1998. The ASW might, however, be susceptible to legal challenge if the reasons that he or she gives are not sufficiently clear and detailed.[27]

5.29 Furthermore, the ASW should ensure that the nearest relative is aware of his or her own right to apply for the patient's admission.[28] If the patient wishes to utilise that right, the ASW should suggest that he or she consult with the relevant doctors.[29]

Application for admission

5.30 As we have seen, where a patient is to be subject to MHA 1983, it is preferable that an application to that effect be made by an ASW. A nearest relative may, however, make application for a patient to be:

- admitted for assessment, under section 2 of MHA 1983 (or, in a case of emergency, under section 4)
- admitted for treatment, under section 3 of MHA 1983[30]
- received into guardianship.[31]

---

24   MHA 1983 *Code of Practice*, para. 2.31.
25   *Ibid.*, paras. 2.21 and 2.32.
26   MHA 1983, s 13(4).
27   MHA 1983 *Code of Practice*, para. 2.32.
28   See paras. **5.30–5.38** and **5.39–5.43**.
29   MHA 1983 *Code of Practice*, para. 2.32.
30   MHA 1983, s 11(1). For MHA 1983, s 2 and a discussion of admission for assessment, see: Jones 2006, paras. 1–029
      to1–039; see also: MHA 1983 *Code of Practice*, Chapter 2 and 5, and MHA 1983 *Memorandum*, paras. 15, 17–19. For MHA
      1983, s 3 and a discussion of admission for treatment, see: Jones 2006, paras. 1–040 to 1–053; see also: MHA 1983
      Memorandum, paras. 16 and 20. For MHA 1983, s 4 and a discussion of admission for assessment in cases of emergency, see:
      Jones 2006, paras. 1–054 to 1–060; see also: MHA 1983 *Code of Practice*, Chapter 6; MHA 1983 *Memorandum*, para. 24.
31   See paras. **5.39–5.43**.

5.31 The nearest relative has no power to make an application for a patient to be subject to aftercare under supervision, under section 25A-J of MHA 1983.[32] In the case of a child-patient who is a ward of court, the nearest relative may only make an application for his or her admission to hospital with leave of the court.[33]

5.32 A nearest relative may not make an admission application unless he or she has personally seen the patient:

- within the last 14 days, if the application is under section 3 of MHA 1983[34] or

- within the last 24 hours, if the application is under section 4.[35]

5.33 A nearest relative will not have 'personally seen' the patient where he or she purports to have done so only through an intermediary.[36] Actual face-to-face contact will be required.

5.34 It seems that this obligation is not the same as the one placed on an ASW who wishes to apply for a patient to be admitted to hospital. The ASW must first 'interview the patient in a suitable manner and satisfy himself that detention in a hospital is in all the circumstances of the case the most appropriate way of providing the care and medical treatment' the patient needs.[37] The Court of Appeal has held that this interview may, but need not, take place when the ASW-applicant 'personally sees' the patient (and so complies with the section 11(5) duty).[38]

5.35 Although he or she might have the power to do so, a nearest relative will not have the *duty* to make an admission application, even though the circumstances may seem to render it appropriate. The nearest relative is therefore in a different position to the ASW, who, if the relevant circumstances exist, *must* make an admission application.[39]

5.36 The forms that a nearest relative must use are as follows:

- for an application for admission for assessment (under section 2 of MHA 1983) – *Form 1*[40]

- for assessment in a case of emergency (under section 4) – *Form 5*[41] and

- for treatment (under section 3) – *Form 8.*[42]

32   MHA 1983, s 25A(5).
33   MHA 1983, s 33(1).
34   MHA 1983, s 11(5).
35   MHA 1983, ss 4(5) and 11(5).
36   *R v South Western Hospital Managers, ex parte M* [1994] 1 All ER 161.
37   MHA 1983, s 13(2). See also: MHA 1983 *Code of Practice*, para. 2.12; MHA 1983 *Memorandum*, para. 34.
38   *Re Whitbread (Mental Patient: Habeas Corpus)* [1997] EWCA Civ 1945, *per* Phillips LJ.
39   MHA 1983, s 13(1).
40   Mental Health (Hospital, Guardianship and Consent to Treatment) Regulations 1983 [Regulations], reg 4(1)(a)(i). (An application by an ASW will be in *Form 2.*)
41   Regulations, reg 4(1)(c)(i). (An application by an ASW will be in *Form 6.*)
42   Regulations, reg 4(1)(e)(i). (An application by an ASW will be in *Form 9.*)

5.37 An application for a patient's admission to hospital under section 2 or 3 of MHA 1983 cannot stand alone. It must be supported by the written medical recommendations of two registered medical practitioners.[43] This is so, even if the application is made by the nearest relative. Each recommendation should state that in the opinion of its author the relevant admission criteria are met.[44] (An application will be treated as having been made under section 4 of MHA 1983 where it is supported by only one such recommendation.)

5.38 If a patient is admitted to hospital under section 2 or section 3 of MHA 1983 upon application by his or her nearest relative, the 'managers' of the hospital must inform the relevant local authority, which will be the one for the area in which the patient resided immediately before his or her admission. (This requirement does not apply where the patient is admitted under section 4, but it probably *should* be fulfilled where a patient's detention, having begun under section 4, continues under section 2.) The authority must then arrange for a social worker to interview the patient and provide a report on his or her social circumstances.[45] The information must be given, and the social worker's interview arranged, as soon as practicable. Any report will be provided to the hospital managers.

Application for guardianship

5.39 Although, as before, an ASW is the preferred applicant, a nearest relative may apply for a patient to be admitted to guardianship under sections 7 and 8 of MHA 1983.[46] (No such application may be made by the nearest relative – or by anyone else – where the patient is a ward of court.[47])

5.40 However, no such application may be made by the nearest relative unless he or she has personally seen the patient within the period of 14 days ending with the date of the application.[48]

5.41 Once again, and as with a hospital admission application, a nearest relative will be under no obligation to make a guardianship application.

5.42 When making a guardianship application, the nearest relative must use *Form 17* (of which he or she must complete Part I).[49]

43   MHA 1983, ss 2(2) and 3(3). The factors to be taken into account when deciding between an application for admission under s 2 and one under s 3 are set out in Chapter 5 of the MHA 1983 *Code of Practice*.
44   As to which, see MHA 1983, ss 2(2) and 3(3) respectively.
45   MHA 1983, s 14. See also MHA 1983 *Memorandum*, para. 37.
46   MHA 1983, s 11(1). See: Jones 2006, paras. 1–085 to 1–114; see also: MHA 1983 *Code of Practice*, Chapter 13; MHA 1983 *Memorandum*, paras. 32–36, 38–42, 85–96, 98 and 106.
47   MHA 1983, s 33(3).
48   MHA 1983, s 11(5).
49   Regulations, reg 5(1)(a)(i).

5.43 An application for a patient's admission to guardianship must be founded upon written medical recommendations in the prescribed form of two registered medical practitioners.[50] This is so, even if the application is made by the nearest relative. Each recommendation should state that in the opinion of its author the relevant admission criteria are met.[51]

Consultation

5.44 In some circumstances, where it is proposed to take certain steps concerning a patient, the nearest relative has the right to be consulted about those steps.

Before an application for admission for treatment

5.45 This is perhaps the best known of the circumstances in which a patient's nearest relative must be consulted.

A DUTY TO CONSULT

5.46 The relevant provision is section 11(4) of MHA 1983, which provides that:

1. an ASW may not make an application for a patient's admission for treatment (under section 3 of MHA 1983) until he or she has consulted the person appearing to be the nearest relative of the patient[52]

2. the nearest relative may object to the application being made, and if he or she does so, the ASW may not proceed with it

3. the duty to consult the nearest relative does not apply if it appears to the ASW that in the circumstances such consultation (a) is not reasonably practicable[53] or (b) would involve unreasonable delay.[54]

5.47 No similar duty exists with regard to a patient's admission for assessment (under section 2 of MHA 1983), and an application to that end may be made by an ASW even without consulting the nearest relative. (Likewise, there will be no section 11(4) duty where the patient concerned is a ward of court.[55])

---

50   MHA 1983, s 7(3).
51   As to which, see MHA 1983, s 7(2).
52   See paras. **5.59–5.62**.
53   See paras. **5.48–5.56**.
54   See paras. **5.57** and **5.58**.
55   MHA 1983, s 33(1).

PRACTICABILITY

5.48 Even where it exists, the section 11(4) duty need not be fulfilled if it appears to the ASW that in the circumstances, consultation is not reasonably practicable.

5.49 It would almost certainly not be 'reasonably practicable' for an ASW to consult a nearest relative:

- where the ASW cannot obtain sufficient information to establish the nearest relative's identity

- where it would require an excessive amount of investigation to identify the nearest relative[56]

- if the nearest relative was incapable of being consulted (for example, by reason of his or her own mental disorder) or

- if the nearest relative had made it clear that he or she did not wish to be consulted.

5.50 In addition, the High Court has accepted that consultation will not be practicable – and will therefore be unnecessary – where there is credible evidence that it would cause a breach of the patient's right to respect for his or her private and family life under Article 8 of the ECHR.[57]

5.51 To guard against this eventuality, an ASW must ask whether consultation, or the knowledge that it was to take place or had taken place, would:

- cause the patient emotional distress or physical harm

- lead to a deterioration in his or her mental health or

- expose him or her to the possibility of financial or other exploitation.

5.52 If consultation *would* have any of the effects described above, it should not take place. This question must be asked, whether or not the patient is capable and/or objecting to the nearest relative being consulted.

5.53 In the case in question, the patient's distress was occasioned by her poor relationship with her nearest relative, which, the court accepted, made it inappropriate for the ASW to consult the latter. In so holding, the court contradicted paragraph 2.16 of the MHA 1983 Code of Practice, which stated that consultation might not be dispensed with merely because it was considered inappropriate. The court said that this paragraph was both 'wrong' and 'contrary to

---

56   MHA 1983 *Code of Practice*, para. 2.16.
57   *R (E) v Bristol City Council* [2005] EWHC 74 (Admin). See paras. **1.80–1.83**.

common sense'.[58] The Department of Health has now issued guidance to the effect that the relevant paragraph has been withdrawn.[59]

5.54 The practice adopted in this case may be seen as a means of circumventing perceived – and acknowledged – difficulties with the nearest relative.[60] It is only a partial solution, however, and although it might relieve the ASW of the duty of consultation, it will not affect the nearest relative's other rights and powers. In any case, there will be few occasions on which the effect of consultation upon the patient will be as detrimental as the court accepted it would be here. The court acknowledged this, stating that the significant role of the nearest relative is not lightly to be removed.[61]

5.55 Consultation should not be dispensed with on grounds of 'practicability' merely because the nearest relative objects to the making of an application. If the nearest relative's objection is unreasonable, an application should be made to the court for an order displacing him or her as nearest relative; if it is not unreasonable, the objection should be allowed to prevail.

5.56 Even if an ASW has not been able to consult the nearest relative before making an application under section 3 of MHA 1983, he or she should continue to try to do so afterwards, if only to inform the nearest relative of his or her power of discharge. If and when the ASW succeeds in giving the nearest relative such information, the ASW must so inform the hospital where the patient is now liable to be detained.[62]

UNREASONABLE DELAY

5.57 The duty to consult the nearest relative also does not apply if it appears to the ASW that in the circumstances such consultation would involve unreasonable delay.

5.58 There is nothing to say at what point a delay becomes unreasonable. Initially, that will be a question for the ASW on the facts of a particular case, but ultimately, it might be one for the court to answer.

---

58   *Ibid.*, at [28].
59   Available at www.dh.gov.uk/PolicyAndGuidance/HealthAndSocialCareTopics/MentalHealth/MentalHealthArticle/fs/
      en?CONTENT_ID=4077674andchk=DB37MW
60   See paras. **1.15–1.21**.
61   *R (E) v Bristol City Council* [2005] EWHC 74 (Admin), at [29].
62   MHA 1983 *Code of Practice*, para. 2.16.

APPEARING TO BE THE NEAREST RELATIVE

5.59 The requirement imposed on the ASW is to consult, not the nearest relative, but the person *appearing to be* the nearest relative of the patient. The two are not necessarily the same.

5.60 The test in this regard is entirely subjective. In other words, it will simply ask whether the person consulted appeared to the ASW to be the patient's nearest relative. It will be irrelevant whether, in forming that view, the ASW acted reasonably.[63] (The latitude afforded to the ASW in this regard is to be contrasted with the somewhat stricter, *objective* standard, by which the court, when invited to displace a nearest relative, will judge the 'reasonableness' of the nearest relative's objection to admission.[64])

5.61 When deciding whether – and if so, *whom* – to consult, an ASW will not have a duty to make reasonable enquiries. It has been said that an ASW need not 'don the mantle of Sherlock Holmes', and that his or her decision will only be susceptible to legal challenge if he or she:

- failed to apply the criteria in section 26 when attempting to determine the patient's nearest relative

- acted in bad faith or

- in some other way reached a conclusion that was plainly wrong.[65]

5.62 An ASW will not, however, have satisfied this requirement if the person he or she consults is, as a matter of law, incapable of being the nearest relative (because, for example, that person is ordinarily resident in the Republic of Ireland).[66]

THE TIMING OF CONSULTATION

5.63 The Act says only that consultation must take place before an application is made; it makes no express provision as to the application's precise timing. It would seem, therefore, that consultation might lawfully take place *before:* (a) the ASW has seen the patient (as he or she is required to do by section 11(5) of MHA 1983); or (b) one or both of the medical recommendations have been obtained.[67] The consultation must, however, relate to the application that is proposed.[68]

63   *Re D (Mental Patient: Habeas Corpus)* [2000] 2 FLR 848, CA.
64   See paras. **4.37–4.41**.
65   *R (WC) v South London and Maudsley NHS Trust and another* [2001] EWHC Admin 1025, *per* Scott Baker J at [27].
66   *R v South Western Hospital Managers, ex parte M* [1994] 1 All ER 161. See paras. **2.48–2.52**.
67   MHA 1983 *Memorandum*, para. 30.
68   *Re Whitbread (Mental Patient: Habeas Corpus)* [1997] EWCA Civ 1945, *per* Phillips LJ.

THE FORM OF CONSULTATION

5.64 Ordinarily, it is desirable for an ASW to consult the nearest relative in a face-to-face meeting. It would seem, however, that there might be the alternative of doing so through an intermediary.[69] Where an intermediary is necessary, it is preferable that the role be performed by another ASW.

5.65 It would seem that the purpose of the consultation is two-fold:

1. to provide information to the ASW to help him or her decide whether to apply for the patient's admission and

2. to put the nearest relative in a position to object to any such application.[70]

5.66 It has been held that the essence of consultation is 'the communication of a genuine invitation to give advice and a genuine consideration of that advice'.[71] Therefore, it will be insufficient for an ASW merely to inform the nearest relative of the proposed application.[72]

5.67 It has further been held that whatever its form, the consultation must be 'full and effective, to ensure that the nearest relative has the opportunity to play his full part in the process'.[73] Therefore, although there is nothing to state that the consultation may not be conducted via correspondence (or, one might add, e-mail or text messaging), it is hard to see how the use of such means would satisfy this requirement.

5.68 The duty to consult is placed on the individual ASW, who will be personally liable for ensuring that it is properly and lawfully performed. Care should be taken, therefore, in communicating with the nearest relative, not to breach the patient's confidentiality in a way that might infringe the common law or the Human Rights Act 1998. That said, an ASW might be susceptible to legal challenge if the information he or she gives to the nearest relative is not sufficiently clear and detailed.

---

69   *R v South Western Hospital Managers, ex parte M* [1994] 1 All ER 161; MHA 1983 *Memorandum*, para. 30.
70   *Re Whitbread (Mental Patient: Habeas Corpus)* [1997] EWCA Civ 1945, *per* Phillips LJ.
71   *R v Secretary of State for Social Services, ex parte Association of Metropolitan Authorities* [1986] 1 All ER 164, *per* Webster J at 167.
72   *Re Briscoe* [1998] EWHC 771 (Admin).
73   *R v South Western Hospital Managers, ex parte M* [1994] 1 All ER 161, *per* Laws J at 175, 176.

OBJECTION

5.69 If the nearest relative objects to a patient's admission under section 3 of MHA 1983 (or for guardianship under section 7), that admission cannot go ahead. (If the objection is unreasonable, that might be a reason for seeking to displace the nearest relative.[74])

5.70 Although an objection by the nearest relative to a patient's admission for treatment under section 3 of MHA 1983 will have significant consequences, the ASW need not expressly invite such an objection.[75]

5.71 If the nearest relative does not object to a section 3 application being made, or if he or she merely 'wishes to sit on the fence', the ASW may proceed with the application.[76] The same is so where the nearest relative withdraws his or her objection. In such circumstances, however, it would be prudent for the ASW who subsequently makes a detention application to obtain written confirmation that the nearest relative's objection has been withdrawn.[77]

5.72 Once a decision has been taken to detain a patient under section 3, it is not open to an ASW to seek to overreach the nearest relative's objection by applying for the patient to be detained under section 2 instead.[78]

5.73 Where an application is, or *is to be*, made for a patient to be admitted, not under section 3 of MHA 1983, but under section 2, the nearest relative has the right to be *informed* – but not *consulted* – about that application. He or she may be so informed either before or after the application is made, and will not have the right to object to it.[79]

Before an application for guardianship

5.74 A nearest relative has the same consultation rights in connection with a guardianship application that he or she has in connection with an application for admission to hospital. Once again, the relevant provision is section 11(4) of MHA 1983, which provides that:

  1. an ASW may not make an application for guardianship (under section 7 of MHA 1983) until he or she has consulted the person appearing to be the nearest relative of the patient[80]

---

74   Under s 29 of MHA 1983, as to which, see paras. **4.35–4.41**.
75   *Re GM (Patient: Consultation)* [2000] MHLR 41.
76   *R (G) v Ealing LBC* [2002] EWHC Admin 1112, *per* Scott Baker J at [10].
77   *Re Shearon* [1996] COD 223, DC, *per* Simon Brown LJ.
78   *R v Wilson, ex parte Williamson* [1996] COD 42.
79   See paras. **5.80–5.88**.
80   See paras. **5.59–5.62**.

2. the nearest relative may object to the application being made, and if he or she does so, the ASW may not proceed with the application

3. the duty to consult the nearest relative does not apply if it appears to the ASW that in the circumstances such consultation (a) is not reasonably practicable[81] or (b) would involve unreasonable delay.[82]

5.75 The same consultation considerations apply to a guardianship application as to an application for a patient's admission to hospital.[83]

Other circumstances

5.76 Save in cases of supervised discharge,[84] there are no other circumstances in which MHA 1983 requires that the nearest relative be consulted. Where, however, a patient is to be transferred, whether to another hospital or to guardianship, it would be good practice for the nearest relative to be consulted about the prospect.[85]

Information

5.77 The nearest relative is entitled to receive various pieces of information, either (a) in his or her own right or (b) on behalf of the patient. The nearest relative's own entitlement is particularly detailed where the patient is – or is to be – subject to supervised discharge.[86]

5.78 But the nearest relative might also be able to demand sight of relevant documents, even where MHA 1983 gives him or her no specific right to do so. The principles that might apply in such circumstances are set out in the concluding paragraphs of this chapter.[87]

The nearest relative in his or her own right

5.79 Under MHA 1983, the nearest relative has certain rights of his or her own to be given information about the course taken with a patient.

---

81 See paras. **5.48–5.56**.
82 See paras. **5.57** and **5.58**.
83 See paras. **5.44–5.73**.
84 As to which, see Chapter 6.
85 MHA 1983 *Memorandum*, para. 84.
86 See Chapter 6.
87 See paras. **5.103–5.110**.

ADMISSION FOR ASSESSMENT

5.80 The nearest relative must be informed of a patient's admission under section 2 (or section 4) of MHA 1983[88] (although, as indicated, he or she has no right to object to such an admission).

5.81 Responsibility for ensuring that this information is provided will rest with the ASW who made – or proposes to make – the relevant application. It will be the ASW's personal responsibility, although, ultimately, he or she may choose to discharge it – and the information may be relayed – via an intermediary.[89]

5.82 The duty of the ASW is not an absolute one, however, and is merely to 'take such steps as are practicable' to provide information to the nearest relative. Although there is no specific authority on the point, use of the word 'practicable' suggests that similar factors apply to this duty as apply to the duty of consultation prior to the making of a section 3 application.[90]

5.83 In fact, according to the Act, the information must be provided, not to the nearest relative, but to the person *appearing to be* the nearest relative. As has been discussed, this is not the same thing.[91] Indeed, it has been held *not* to invalidate a patient's admission under section 2 of MHA 1983 for the relevant information to be given to someone who, though the ASW genuinely believed her to be so, was not the patient's nearest relative.[92]

5.84 In any case, the information need only be provided 'before or within a reasonable time after the application', and so, this is not the same as the right to be consulted *before* – and even to veto – an application for a patient's admission under section 3 of MHA 1983.[93]

5.85 It has been suggested that information provided to the nearest relative more than 24 hours after a patient's detention would not have been provided 'within a reasonable time'.[94] Much, however, will depend on the circumstances, and it is perhaps unwise to be too prescriptive.

5.86 Where, having begun pursuant to section 4 of MHA 1983, a patient's detention continues under section 2, it is likely that the obligation of the relevant ASW will be two-fold, and that he or she will have to provide information to the nearest relative on both occasions. (It might, perhaps, be argued that it would be 'reasonable' in those circumstances for the ASW to postpone the giving of the

88   MHA 1983, s 11(3).
89   *R v South Western Hospital Managers, ex parte M* [1994] 1 All ER 161.
90   See paras. **5.48–5.56**.
91   See paras. **5.59–5.62**.
92   *R v Birmingham Mental Health Trust, ex parte Phillips*, CO/1501/95, 25 May 1995, Tucker J.
93   MHA 1983, s 11(4). See paras. **5.69–5.73**.
94   Jones 2006, paras. 1–121.

information until the patient was detained substantively under section 2. If no such substantive detention took place, however, and the 72 hours of the patient's section 4 detention expired without such information having been given to the nearest relative, it is likely that the ASW would have failed in his or her duty under section 11(3) of MHA 1983.)

5.87 There is nothing in MHA 1983 to require that the relevant information be in writing, and it is likely that the ASW may provide it to the nearest relative verbally.

5.88 As well as informing the nearest relative of a patient's admission under section 2 of MHA 1983, the ASW must also inform the nearest relative of his or her right, under section 23(2)(a) of MHA 1983, to order the patient's discharge from detention.

RE-CLASSIFICATION

5.89 A patient may be detained under section 2 of MHA 1983 where, among other things, he or she is suffering from 'mental disorder'.[95] The Act recognises four classes of mental disorder: mental illness; mental impairment; severe mental impairment; and psychopathic disorder. In order for a patient to be detained under section 3 or admitted to guardianship under section 7, it must be possible, among other things, to reduce the patient's mental disorder to one (or more) of these classes, and an application under either of these sections must state from which class(es) of mental disorder the patient is suffering.[96] But that statement need not be final, and it is possible for a patient who had been thought to suffer from one class of mental disorder subsequently to be re-classified.[97] The patient's Responsible Medical Officer (RMO) is the person who will re-classify him or her.

5.90 The nearest relative has the right to be informed whenever the RMO furnishes a report to 'the managers' the effect of which is to re-classify the patient.[98]

The amended Act

There will be a single, simplified definition of 'mental disorder' and the four existing classes will be abolished. Therefore, there will be no prospect of a patient being re-classified, and neither the patient nor the nearest relative will require substantive rights in that regard.

---

95   MHA 1983, s 2(2).
96   MHA 1983, ss 3(3) and 7(3).
97   MHA 1983, s 16. See: Jones 2006, paras. 1–162 to 1–168; MHA 1983 *Memorandum*, paras. 64–66.
98   MHA 1983, s 16(4).

DISCHARGE

5.91 A patient who is subject to MHA 1983 may be discharged by the nearest relative,[99] but also by his or her RMO,[100] by the managers of the hospital (if he or she is liable to be detained) or the relevant local authority (if he or she is subject to guardianship),[101] or by a MHRT.[102]

5.92 Where a patient is to be discharged otherwise than by his or her nearest relative, the managers must 'take such steps as are practicable' to inform the nearest relative of the patient's discharge.[103]

5.93 Although there is no specific authority on the point, use of the word 'practicable' suggests that similar factors apply to this duty as apply to the duty of consultation prior to the making of a section 3 application.[104]

5.94 In fact, according to the Act, consultation must be with, not the nearest relative, but the person *appearing to be* the nearest relative. As has been indicated, this is not necessarily the same thing.[105]

5.95 Such information shall, 'if practicable', be given at least seven days before the date of discharge.[106]

5.96 It is good practice for the information given to the nearest relative to include details of any care the patient will receive once he or she has left hospital.[107]

5.97 This obligation does not, however, apply if either the patient or the nearest relative has informed the managers that such information should *not* be given.[108] Therefore, it would seem that the patient has an absolute veto on news of his discharge being given to the nearest relative.

The nearest relative on behalf of the patient

5.98 In addition – and, crucially, subject to the wishes of the patient – a nearest relative has the right to be furnished with a copy of any of the following information that is supplied to the patient:

---

99   See paras. **7.6–7.16**.
100 MHA 1983, s 23(2)(a) or (b). See: Jones 2006, paras. 1–257 to 1–266; MHA 1983 *Code of Practice*, Chapter 23; MHA 1983 *Memorandum*, paras. 102–106.
101 MHA 1983, s 23(2)(a).
102 MHA 1983, s 72.
103 MHA 1983, s 133(1).
104 See paras. **5.48–5.56**.
105 See paras. **5.59–5.62**.
106 MHA 1983, s 133(1).
107 MHA 1983 *Code of Practice*, para. 14.3.
108 MHA 1983, s 133(2).

- under which provisions of MHA 1983 the patient is currently detained, and the effect of those provisions upon him or her[109]

- what rights of applying to a MHRT are available to the patient in respect of his or her detention[110]

- the effect of the power, in section 23 of MHA 1983, to discharge a patient (including the power possessed by his or her nearest relative)[111]

- the effect of the RMO's power, in section 25 of MHA 1983, to bar a discharge ordered by the nearest relative, and the effect of the nearest relative's corresponding right to apply to the MHRT under section 66(1)(g)[112]

- the effect of the consent to treatment provisions in Part IV of MHA 1983[113]

- the implications for the patient of the provisions in the MHA 1983 Code of Practice[114]

- the effect of the provisions, in section 120 of MHA 1983, dealing with the investigation of complaints by, or in respect of, detained patients[115]

- the effect of the provisions, in section 134 of MHA 1983, concerning the correspondence of detained patients.[116]

5.99 It should be noted that the right of the nearest relative to be given copies of this information is ancillary to that of patient to receive it in the first place. If the information is never supplied to the patient, it need not be supplied to the nearest relative.

5.100 Responsibility for ensuring that this information is provided will rest with the managers of the hospital in which the patient is detained.

5.101 The right of the nearest relative to receive this information is contingent upon the patient's consent. If, and so far as, the patient objects, the information must not be given to the nearest relative.[117] Therefore, and again, it would seem that the patient has an absolute veto, which he or she may use to prevent the giving of this information to the nearest relative.

109   MHA 1983, s 132(1)(a).
110   MHA 1983, s 132(1)(b).
111   MHA 1983, s 132(2).
112   Ibid.
113   Ibid.
114   Ibid.
115   Ibid.
116   Ibid.
117   MHA 1983, s 132(4).

5.102 If the patient does not object, copies of the information must be given to the nearest relative when the information is given to the patient or within a reasonable time thereafter.[118] (It is, of course, the case that the relevant information must be given to the patient 'as soon as practicable after the commencement' of his or her detention.[119])

The Data Protection Act 1998

5.103 These are all specific rights to information. Where they do not apply, however, it is possible that a nearest relative will be able to use the more general rights contained in the Data Protection Act 1998 (DPA 1998), and that those rights might enable him or her to obtain information in circumstances not envisaged in MHA 1983.

5.104 For the purposes of DPA 1998, information about a patient, his or her medical condition, social circumstances and (if appropriate) detention status is likely to be both 'personal data' and 'sensitive personal data'.[120] This is because it relates to his or her 'physical or mental health or condition'. The processing of such data – by, for example, disclosing it to another person (such as the nearest relative) or another body – is permissible where it is necessary:

- in order to protect the vital interests of the data subject (or another person), where he or she cannot give consent to disclosure and no such consent can be given on his or her behalf[121]

- for the purpose of, or in connection with, any legal proceedings (including prospective legal proceedings)

- for the purpose of obtaining legal advice

- for the purposes of establishing, exercising or defending legal rights[122]

- for the administration of justice, or for the exercise of any functions conferred on any person by or under an enactment.[123]

5.105 However, on its own DPA 1998 might be of little assistance to a nearest relative, for although it *permits* the disclosure of information in these circumstances, it does not *require* it.[124] It would seem to add little or nothing to the specific rights contained in MHA 1983.

118   *Ibid.*
119   MHA 1983, s 132(1) and (2).
120   DPA 1998, s 2(e).
121   DPA 1998, Schedule 3, para. 3.
122   DPA 1998, Schedule 3, para. 6.
123   DPA 1998, Schedule 3, para. 7.
124   See, for example *R (Stevens) v Plymouth City Council and another* [2002] EWCA Civ 388, *per* Hale LJ at [27].

5.106 Therefore, when deciding whether to grant disclosure to the nearest relative in circumstances not covered by MHA 1983, a public authority (such as a NHS body or a social services authority) or an ASW will have to:

1. consider their obligations, both under the common law and under the Human Rights Act 1998 and

2. strike a balance between the public and private interests in maintaining the confidentiality of the information in question and the public and private interests in permitting its disclosure.[125]

The common law

5.107 Health care and social care practitioners owe a duty of confidence to those for whom they care. Although the nature and extent of that duty are beyond the scope of this book,[126] several basic principles may be set out.[127]

- Even though a particular relationship – such as that between a doctor, nurse or social worker and a MHA 1983 patient – might give rise to a duty of confidence, that duty does not cover all the information produced or discovered in the course of the relationship. Among the information that might not be confidential are straightforward descriptions of everyday life.[128]

- Even though the duty of confidence might apply, information that it covers may be disclosed for the purposes for which it was brought into existence. So, for example, medical recommendations provided in support of an application under MHA 1983 will have to be disclosed to the ASW who is to make that application. Without such disclosure, the ASW would be unable to fulfil his or her statutory function. There might be circumstances in which, in seeking disclosure not specifically permitted by MHA 1983, a nearest relative might make a similar claim.[129]

- Even where it exists, a duty of confidence will be overridden where there is a strong public interest in disclosure.[130] This is so, even where

---

125   *Ibid., per* Hale LJ at [32].
126   But see: Montgomery 2001, Chapter 11; Kennedy and Grubb 2000, Chapter 7 and 8.
127   *R (Stevens) v Plymouth City Council and another* [2002] EWCA Civ 388, *per* Hale LJ at [33]–[51].
128   *Ibid., per* Hale LJ at [33].
129   *Ibid., per* Hale LJ at [34]. See also *W v Egdell* [1990] Ch 359, *per* Bingham LJ at 419c.
130   *R (Stevens) v Plymouth City Council and another* [2002] EWCA Civ 388, *per* Hale LJ at [35]. See also *W v Egdell* [1990] Ch 359, *per* Bingham LJ at 419e.

a patient (for example) is capable and refuses to consent to such disclosure.[131]

The European Convention on Human Rights

5.108 The principles underlying the common law duty of confidence are reinforced by the European Convention on Human Rights (ECHR), and in particular, by Article 6 of the ECHR (the right to a fair trial) and Article 8 (the right to respect for one's private and family life).

5.109 It is worth noting, however, that these ECHR provisions are not all-embracing.[132]

- Although Article 6 is absolute, it has been held that the *elements* of a fair trial are not, and that limitations may be imposed upon them if there is a clear and proper public objective for doing so, and if those limitations are no greater than the situation demands.[133]

- Disclosure might breach Article 8 and still be lawful, provided it is: (a) in accordance with (domestic) law; (b) necessary for one of a number of purposes (such as the protection either of health or morals, or of the rights and freedoms of others); and (c) proportionate to the end it sought to achieve.

- In fact, Article 8 might actually *require* disclosure, because a family member (including one who is a nearest relative) has a right to be involved in the decision-making process.[134]

5.110 It is likely, therefore, that a nearest relative to whom MHA 1983 does not give a specific right in that regard may still claim disclosure of documents that are necessary if he or she is properly to exercise his or her rights and discharge his or her functions, whether under that Act or under other, analogous provisions.

---

131   *R (Stevens) v Plymouth City Council and another* [2002] EWCA Civ 388, *per* Hale LJ at [49]. See also *W v Egdell* [1990] Ch 359.
132   *R (Stevens) v Plymouth City Council and another* [2002] EWCA Civ 388, *per* Hale LJ at [37].
133   *Brown v Stott* [2001] 2 WLR 817, at p.836.
134   *R (Stevens) v Plymouth City Council and another* [2002] EWCA Civ 388, *per* Hale LJ at [46]. See also: *W v United Kingdom* (1977) 10 EHRR 29; *McMichael v United Kingdom* (1995) 20 EHRR 205; *TP and KM v United Kingdom* [2001] 2 FCR 289.

6

Supervised Discharge and the Nearest Relative

This chapter considers the powers of the nearest relative where a patient is subject to supervised discharge. Those powers are at least as numerous as – even if they are no more significant than – the powers granted to the nearest relative elsewhere in MHA 1983.

Introduction

6.1 Where a patient is subject to supervised discharge under the Mental Health Act 1983 (MHA 1983), he or she will have a nearest relative.[1] (If the patient is also a ward of court, any powers the nearest relative might possess will only be exercisable with the permission of the court.[2])

6.2 Supervised discharge is more formally known as 'aftercare under supervision'. It is available in the case of patients who, having been detained under section 3 (or section 37) of MHA 1983, are discharged from detention and leave hospital.[3] Its purpose is to enable such patients to be subjected to formal supervision, even in the community.[4] In truth, the requirements that may be imposed upon patients as part of their supervised discharge are relatively modest.[5]

6.3 In 1995, in the form of a supplement to the MHA 1983 Code of Practice, the Department of Health and the Welsh Office issued detailed guidance on supervised discharge.[6]

---

1   MHA 1983, s 26(3) and (1).
2   MHA 1983, s 33(4).
3   MHA 1983, s 25A-J. See: Jones 2006, paras. 1–283 to 1–408; Department of Health and Welsh Office, *Mental Health Act 1983 Code of Practice*, 1999 [MHA 1983 *Code of Practice*], Chapter 28; Department of Health, *Mental Health Act 1983: Memorandum on Parts I to VI, VIII and X*, 1995, HMSO [MHA 1983 *Memorandum*], paras. 113–140.
4   MHA 1983 *Memorandum*, para. 113.
5   MHA 1983, s 25D(3).
6   Department of Health and Welsh Office 1995, *Mental Health (Patients in the Community) Act 1995 – Guidance on supervised discharge (Aftercare under Supervision) and Related Provisions* [Guidance on supervised discharge].

The amended Act

The Government proposes to abolish supervised discharge.[7] In its place, there is to be supervised community treatment (SCT).[8] It would seem that where a patient is subject to SCT, the nearest relative will have none of the rights currently attached to supervised discharge.

6.4 An application for supervised discharge will be made by the Responsible Medical Officer (RMO), while the patient is still liable to be detained in hospital. Once he or she has left hospital and become subject to supervised discharge, a patient will have: (1) a supervisor (who will often be a social worker); and (2) a community RMO (who will be a doctor).

6.5 Where a patient is – or is to be – subject to supervised discharge, the nearest relative will have the right in certain circumstances:

1. to be consulted and

2. to be given certain information.

Consultation

6.6 Under MHA 1983, a nearest relative may have the right to be consulted:

- before a supervision application is made and

- whenever supervised discharge is to be modified, renewed or brought to an end.

Before a supervision application is made

6.7 An application for a patient to be subject to supervised discharge is known as a 'supervision application'.

6.8 The nearest relative, among others, must be consulted before a supervision application is made.[9] The patient's RMO will be responsible for ensuring that this consultation takes place (although, strictly speaking, there is nothing to require the RMO to conduct it in person).

---

7   Department of Health and Home Office, *Mental Health Bill*, November 2006, HL Bill 1 54/2 [MHB 2006], cl 29(2).
8   *Ibid.*, cl 25–28.
9   MHA 1983, s 25B(2)(b).

6.9 This requirement might not apply, however, if the patient has requested that there be no consultation.[10] In such circumstances, the nearest relative must not be consulted unless:

- the patient has a propensity to violent or dangerous behaviour towards others[11] and

- the RMO considers it appropriate for there to be consultation with the (person appearing to be the) nearest relative about the making of the supervision application.[12]

6.10 In this regard, the guidance states: 'The patient's objection should not lightly be set aside', and that among the matters the RMO is likely to wish to consider in this regard are:

- the seriousness of any past violence by the patient

- against whom any such violence has been directed

- how the patient has responded to treatment and

- how far consultation with the nearest relative is likely to help in the assessment of the patient's present condition and needs.[13]

6.11 **Carers:** Even if the need to consult the nearest relative is removed in this way, it will still apply if the person who happens to be the nearest relative is also an informal carer of the patient.[14] MHA 1983 states that as well as the nearest relative, the RMO must consult 'any person [whom he or she] believes will play a substantial part in the care of the patient after he leaves hospital but will not be professionally concerned with any of the aftercare services to be so provided'.[15] This is quite separate from the requirement to consult the nearest relative and, unlike that requirement, cannot be dispensed with at the patient's request.

6.12 Any consultation must be with, not the nearest relative, but the person *appearing to be* the nearest relative. As has been discussed, this is not necessarily the same thing.[16]

6.13 The obligation concerning the nearest relative is not absolute: it is simply to take 'such steps as are practicable' to consult him or her. Use of the word 'practicable' suggests that similar factors apply to this duty as apply to the duty of consultation prior to the making of a section 3 application.[17] This means that a

10   MHA 1983, s 25B(3).
11   MHA 1983, s 25B(3)(a).
12   MHA 1983, s 25B(3)(b); MHA 1983 *Memorandum*, para. 118.
13   *Guidance on supervised discharge*, para. 27.
14   *Guidance on supervised discharge*, para. 21.
15   MHA 1983, s 25B(2)(a)(iv).
16   See paras. **5.59–5.62**.
17   See paras. **5.48–5.56**.

RMO may – and probably *should* – conclude that consultation would be impracticable, and therefore should not take place, where:

- the nearest relative is incapable of being consulted (for example, by reason of his or her own mental disorder)

- the nearest relative has said that he or she does not wish to be consulted

- there is credible evidence that consultation would breach the patient's right to respect for his or her private and family life under Article 8 of the ECHR[18]

- consultation, or the knowledge that it is to take place or had taken place, would cause the patient emotional distress or physical harm, lead to a deterioration in his or her mental health, or expose him or her to the possibility of financial or other exploitation.

6.14 Unlike the one concerning the nearest relative, the obligation to consult a patient's informal carer *is* an absolute one, and it will not be discharged merely by the taking of such steps as are practicable.[19]

6.15 The RMO will have to take into account any views expressed by the nearest relative (or carer).[20] Any such views will not, of course, be binding upon the RMO, who will be free to take steps that were not supported by – and that might, in fact, be contrary to – the views expressed by the consultee. A consultee must, however, be named in any subsequent supervision application.[21]

6.16 According to the guidance:

- although the RMO may delegate the performing of the consultation, he or she will be responsible for ensuring that it is performed, and also for the way it is performed

- a consultee 'must be given a genuine opportunity to comment on the proposed arrangements'

- a consultee should be able to speak to the RMO (or to anyone the RMO has delegated to perform the consultation) alone, if he or she so wishes[22]

- the consultee should be consulted in a suitable and sensitive manner, with recourse to a trained interpreter (for example) where required.[23]

18   *R (E) v Bristol City Council* [2005] EWHC 74 (Admin).
19   MHA 1983, s 25B(2)(a)(iv).
20   MHA 1983, s 25B(2)(c); *Guidance on supervised discharge*, para. 23.
21   MHA 1983, s 25B(5)(e)(ii).
22   *Guidance on supervised discharge*, para. 25
23   *Ibid.*, para. 26. See also MHA 1983 *Code of Practice*, Chapter 2.

UNREASONABLE DELAY

6.17 There is nothing in the provisions concerning supervised discharge to excuse the RMO from consulting where such would involve unreasonable delay. This is to be contrasted with the position that obtains where an application is to be made for a patient's admission for treatment, or for his or her reception into guardianship.[24]

THE FORM OF CONSULTATION

6.18 Similarly, there is nothing to say that the law on the *form* of pre-detention (or pre-guardianship) consultation is of wider application.[25] Nevertheless, it is possible that the law – which, of course, derives, not from MHA 1983 itself, but from the courts' interpretation of its provisions – would be held also to apply to the relevant supervised discharge processes.

Before a modification of supervised discharge

6.19 The nearest relative, among others, must also be consulted before there is any modification in either:

1. the aftercare services provided to a patient who is subject to supervised discharge[26] or

2. any requirements imposed upon him or her.[27]

6.20 This requirement might not apply, however, if the patient has requested that there be no consultation.[28] In such circumstances, the nearest relative must not be consulted unless:

- the patient has a propensity to violent or dangerous behaviour towards others[29] and

- it is considered appropriate for there to be consultation with the (person appearing to be the) nearest relative about the making of the supervision application.[30]

6.21 Carers: Even if the need to consult the nearest relative is removed in this way, it will still apply if the person who happens to be the nearest relative is also an informal carer of the patient.[31] MHA 1983 states that as well as with the nearest

---

24   See paras. **5.57** and **5.58**.
25   See paras. **5.64–5.68**.
26   MHA 1983, s 25E(5); MHA 1983 *Memorandum*, para. 129.
27   MHA 1983, s 25E(6)(c); MHA 1983 *Memorandum*, para. 129.
28   MHA 1983, s 25E(7).
29   MHA 1983, s 25E(7)(a).
30   MHA 1983, s 25E(7)(b). For the factors that might be taken into account, see para. **6.11**.
31   *Guidance on supervised discharge*, para. 21.

relative, there must also be consultation with 'any person [who it is believed] plays (or will play) a substantial part in the care of the patient but is not (or will not be) professionally concerned with the after-care services provided for the patient under section 117 [of MHA 1983]'.[32] This is quite separate from the requirement to consult the nearest relative and, unlike that requirement, cannot be dispensed with at the patient's request.

6.22 In fact, any consultation must be with , not the nearest relative, but the person *appearing to be* the nearest relative. As has been discussed, this is not necessarily the same thing.[33]

6.23 Again, the requirement is simply to take 'such steps as are practicable [...] to consult the person (if any) appearing to be the nearest relative of the patient about the modifications'.[34] As in the provisions dealing with the *making* of a supervision application, this suggests that similar factors apply here as to the duty of consultation in connection with a section 3 application.[35]

6.24 And again, the obligation to consult a patient's informal carer *is* an absolute one.[36]

6.25 Any consultation will be by 'the responsible after-care bodies',[37] which will have to take into account any views expressed by the nearest relative.[38] It would seem that the guidance concerning consultation applies equally here as in any other aspect of supervised discharge.[39]

Before renewal of supervised discharge

6.26 The nearest relative, among others, must also be consulted before a patient's supervised discharge is renewed. Any consultation will be by the community RMO.[40]

6.27 This requirement might not apply, however, if the patient has requested that there be no consultation.[41] In such circumstances, the nearest relative must not be consulted unless:

---

32   MHA 1983, s 25E(6)(b).
33   See paras. **5.59–5.62**.
34   MHA 1983, s 25E(6)(c).
35   See paras. **5.48–5.56** and **6.14**.
36   MHA 1983, s 25E(6)(b).
37   MHA 1983, s 25E(5).
38   MHA 1983, s 25E(6)(d).
39   See para. **6.16**.
40   MHA 1983, s 25G(5)(b).
41   MHA 1983, s 25G(6).

- the patient has a propensity to violent or dangerous behaviour towards others[42] and

- it is considered appropriate for there to be consultation with the (person appearing to be the) nearest relative about the making of the supervision application.[43]

6.28 Carers: Even if the need to consult the nearest relative is removed in this way, it will still apply if the person who happens to be the nearest relative is also an informal carer of the patient.[44] MHA 1983 states that as well as with the nearest relative, there must also be consultation with 'any person [whom it is believed] plays a substantial part in the care of the patient but is not professionally concerned with the after-care services so provided'.[45] This is quite separate from the requirement to consult the nearest relative and, unlike that requirement, cannot be dispensed with at the patient's request.

6.29 In fact, any consultation must be with, not the nearest relative, but the person *appearing to be* the nearest relative. As has been indicated, this is not necessarily the same thing.[46]

6.30 The requirement, which will apply before consideration is given under section 25G(3) of MHA 1983 as to whether the grounds are met for a patient's supervised discharge to be renewed, is actually take 'such steps as are practicable [...] to consult the person (if any) appearing to be the nearest relative of the patient'.[47] Again, this use of the word 'practicable' suggests that similar factors apply here as apply to the duty of consultation in connection with a section 3 application.[48]

6.31 Once again, the obligation to consult a patient's informal carer *is* an absolute one.[49]

6.32 Having consulted, the community RMO will have to take into account any relevant views expressed by the nearest relative (or carer).[50] Within the provisions for supervised discharge, this is the only occasion upon which the views required to be taken into account are confined to *relevant* ones. The use of the word 'relevant' might be a drafting error, or it might be deliberate. It suggests, however, that, having solicited the views of the nearest relative, the community RMO may dismiss some or all of them – and not, in fact, take them into account – on the

---

42   MHA 1983, s 25G(6)(a).
43   MHA 1983, s 25G(6)(b). For the factors that might be taken into account, see para. **6.13**.
44   *Guidance on supervised discharge*, para. 21.
45   MHA 1983, s 25G(5)(a)(v).
46   See paras. **5.59–5.62**.
47   MHA 1983, s 25G(5)(b); MHA 1983 *Memorandum*, para. 135.
48   See paras. **5.48–5.56** and **6.14**.
49   MHA 1983, s 25G(5)(a)(v).
50   MHA 1983, s 25G(5)(c).

grounds that they are not relevant. (A community RMO who took such a course would be well advised to record it, and the rationale for it, very carefully.)

6.33 It would seem that the guidance concerning consultation applies equally here as in any other aspect of supervised discharge.[51]

Before ending supervised discharge

6.34 The nearest relative, among others, must also be consulted before supervised discharge is brought to an end. Consultation will be by the patient's community RMO.[52]

6.35 This requirement might not apply, however, if the patient has requested that there be no consultation.[53] In such circumstances, the nearest relative must not be consulted unless:

- the patient has a propensity to violent or dangerous behaviour towards others[54] and

- the community RMO considers that it is appropriate for there to be consultation with the (person appearing to be the) nearest relative about the making of the supervision application.[55]

6.36 Carers: Even if the need to consult the nearest relative is removed in this way, it will still apply if the person who happens to be the nearest relative is also an informal carer of the patient.[56] MHA 1983 states that as well as with the nearest relative, there must also be consultation with 'any person [who it is believed] plays a substantial part in the care of the patient but is not professionally concerned with the after-care services so provided'.[57] This is quite separate from the requirement to consult the nearest relative and, unlike that requirement, cannot be dispensed with at the patient's request.

6.37 In fact, according to the Act, any consultation must be with, not the nearest relative, but the person *appearing to be* the nearest relative. As has been indicated, this is not necessarily the same thing.[58]

6.38 The requirement, which will apply before a direction is given that a patient is to cease to be subject to supervised discharge, is to take 'such steps as are practicable [...] to consult the person (if any) appearing to be the nearest relative of the

---

51   See para. **6.16**.
52   MHA 1983, s 25H(3)(b).
53   MHA 1983, s 25H(4).
54   MHA 1983, s 25H(4)(a).
55   MHA 1983, s 25H(4)(b). For the factors that might be taken into account, see para. **6.13**.
56   *Guidance on supervised discharge*, para. 21.
57   MHA 1983, s 25H(3)(a)(v).
58   See paras. **5.59–5.62**.

patient about the giving of the direction'.[59] Again, this use of the word 'practicable' suggests that similar factors apply here as apply to the duty of consultation in connection with a section 3 application.[60]

6.39 Once more, the obligation to consult a patient's informal carer *is* an absolute one.[61]

6.40 Having consulted, the community RMO will have to take into account any views – and not just any *relevant* views – expressed by the nearest relative (or carer).[62] It would seem that the guidance concerning consultation applies equally here as in any other aspect of supervised discharge.[63]

Information

6.41 Under MHA 1983, a nearest relative may have the right to be given information about:

1. the making of a supervision application
2. any planned modification to supervised discharge
3. a change in the patient's community RMO or supervisor
4. the re-classification of the patient
5. the renewal of supervised discharge and
6. the ending of supervised discharge.

Making a supervision application

6.42 As has been discussed, a nearest relative might have certain consultation rights in connection with the making of a supervision application.[64]

6.43 If he or she was consulted about the making of a supervision application, the nearest relative, among others, must be given certain information when that application comes to be made.[65] The information, which must be given in writing, is:

- that the application is being made
- the aftercare services that are to be provided to the patient under section 117 of MHA 1983

---

59   MHA 1983, s 25H(3)(b); MHA 1983 *Memorandum*, para. 138.
60   See paras. **5.48–5.56** and **6.14**.
61   MHA 1983, s 25H(3)(a)(v).
62   MHA 1983, s 25H(3)(c).
63   See para. **6.16**.
64   See paras. **6.7–6.18**.
65   MHA 1983, s 25B(10); MHA 1983 *Memorandum*, para. 125.

- any requirements that are to be imposed upon the patient under section 25D of MHA 1983 and
- the names of the patient's community RMO and supervisor.[66]

6.44 If the patient vetoed consultation, the nearest relative must not be informed that a supervision application has been made.

6.45 The information might still have to be given to the person who is the nearest relative, however, if he or she was consulted about the making of the supervision application, not as the nearest relative, but because he or she gives informal care to the patient.[67] As has been discussed, the patient would not have been able to veto such a consultation.

Modifying supervised discharge

6.46 The conditions that apply to a patient may be modified while ever he or she is subject to supervised discharge.[68] As we have seen, the nearest relative has certain consultation rights in connection with any such modification.[69]

6.47 If the nearest relative was consulted about any modification in either (a) the aftercare services provided to a patient subject to supervised discharge or (b) any requirements imposed on the patient under section 25D of MHA 1983, he or she must be informed in writing that they have been so modified.[70] (There is nothing to require that this information be given orally as well.)

6.48 If the patient vetoed consultation, then, again, the nearest relative must not be informed that supervised discharge has been modified. However, a person who was not consulted as nearest relative might nevertheless have been consulted because he or she provided the patient with informal care. If so, that person will have to be informed about the modifying of supervised discharge after all.[71]

Changing the CRMO or Supervisor

6.49 A patient's community RMO or supervisor may be changed while he or she remains subject to supervised discharge.[72]

---

66   MHA 1983, s 25B(11). See also *Guidance on supervised discharge*, paras. 37 and 38.
67   MHA 1983, s 25B(10)(b).
68   MHA 1983, s 25E(1).
69   See paras. **6.19–6.25**.
70   MHA 1983, s 25E(8)(c); MHA 1983 *Memorandum*, para. 130.
71   MHA 1983, s 25E(11)(b).
72   MHA 1983, s 25E(9) and (10).

6.50 The nearest relative must be informed in writing of any such change; or rather, the responsible aftercare bodies must 'take such steps as are practicable' so to inform him or her.[73] Use of the word 'practicable' again suggests that similar factors apply to this duty as to the duty of consultation prior to the making of a section 3 application.[74]

6.51 In fact, the information must be provided, not to the nearest relative, but to the person *appearing to be* the nearest relative. As has been discussed, this is not the same thing.[75]

6.52 The patient may veto the giving of such information to the nearest relative.[76] If he or she does so, the information must not be given to the nearest relative. This is so, even if the patient has violent or dangerous propensities. This position is therefore to be distinguished from the one that obtains prior to the making of a supervision application, or to the renewal or ending of supervised discharge, when the patient's veto may be overridden.

6.53 Even if the patient vetoes the giving of information about a change to the community RMO or supervisor, the person who happens to be the nearest relative might still be entitled to receive such information if he or she is also an informal carer of the patient.[77]

Re-classification

6.54 While subject to supervised discharge, a patient classified as suffering from one form of mental disorder may be re-classified as suffering from a different (or additional) form of mental disorder.[78]

6.55 Where a report whose effect is to re-classify the patient in this way is furnished to the managers, the nearest relative must be informed in writing that it has been so furnished. Or rather, the responsible aftercare bodies must 'take such steps as are practicable' so to inform him or her.[79] (There is nothing to require that this information be given orally as well.) Once more, use of the word 'practicable' suggests that similar factors apply to this duty as to the duty of consultation prior to the making of a section 3 application.[80]

73   MHA 1983, s 25E(9)–(11).
74   See paras. **5.48–5.56** and **6.14**.
75   See paras. **5.59–5.62**.
76   MHA 1983, s 25E(11)(c).
77   MHA 1983, s 25E(11)(b).
78   MHA 1983, s 25F(1).
79   MHA 1983, s 25F(1) and (4)(b); MHA 1983 *Memorandum*, para. 134.
80   See paras. **5.48–5.56** and **6.14**.

6.56 The information must be provided, not to the nearest relative, but to the person *appearing to be* the nearest relative. As has been discussed, this is not the same thing.[81]

6.57 The patient may veto the giving of such information to the nearest relative.[82] If he or she does so, the veto will again be absolute, and the information must not be given to the nearest relative.[83]

6.58 Even if the nearest relative also provides informal care, he or she will not be entitled to receive information about the re-classifying of the patient on that ground alone; if the patient vetoes the giving of such information, the nearest relative will have no other right to receive it.

Renewal

6.59 A patient's supervised discharge will last for a period of six months, but during that period it may be renewed, first for a further six months, and then for successive periods of 12 months. Renewal will take place when the community RMO furnishes to the responsible aftercare bodies a report to that effect.

6.60 As has been discussed, the nearest relative has certain consultation rights in connection with the renewal of supervised discharge.[84] If those rights were respected and he or she was consulted in that regard, the nearest relative must be informed in writing when the community RMO has furnished a renewal report to the managers.[85] (There is nothing to require that this information be given orally as well.)

6.61 If the patient vetoed consultation, the nearest relative must not be informed that supervised discharge has been renewed. That information might still have to be given to the nearest relative, however, if he or she was consulted about renewal, not as the nearest relative, but because he or she had given the patient informal care.[86] As has been discussed, the patient would not have been able to veto such a consultation.

Ending supervised discharge

6.62 Where a patient ceases to be subject to supervised discharge, the nearest relative must be informed of that fact in writing; or rather, the responsible after-

---

81   See paras. **5.59–5.62**.
82   MHA 1983, s 25F(4)(b).
83   See also para. **6.48**.
84   See paras. **6.26–6.33**.
85   MHA 1983, s 25G(8)(c); MHA 1983 *Memorandum*, para. 137.
86   MHA 1983, s 25G(8)(b).

care bodies must 'take such steps as are practicable' so to inform him or her.[87] (There is nothing to require that this information be given orally as well.) Use of the word 'practicable' once again suggests that similar factors apply to this duty as to the duty of consultation prior to the making of a section 3 application.[88]

6.63 In fact, the requisite information must be provided, not to the nearest relative, but to the person *appearing to be* the nearest relative. As has been discussed, this is not the same thing.[89]

6.64 The patient may, however, request that such information is not given to the nearest relative.[90] On this occasion, however, the patient will not have a veto, and information may still be given to the nearest relative if:

- the patient has a propensity to violent or dangerous behaviour towards others[91] and

- the community RMO considers that it is appropriate for the (person appearing to be the) nearest relative to be informed that the patient has ceased to be subject to supervised discharge.[92]

6.65 Even if the giving of information about the bringing to an end of supervised discharge is vetoed in this way, the person who is the nearest relative might still be entitled to receive that information if he or she provides the patient with informal care.[93]

---

87   MHA 1983, s 25H(6)(c); MHA 1983 *Memorandum*, para. 138.
88   See paras. **5.48–5.56** and **6.14**.
89   See paras. **5.59–5.62**.
90   MHA 1983, s 25H(7).
91   MHA 1983, s 25H(4)(a).
92   MHA 1983, s 25H(4)(b).
93   MHA 1983, s 25H(6)(b).

7

Discharge
and the Nearest Relative

This chapter discusses the circumstances in which a nearest relative might bring about a patient's discharge from detention.

Introduction

7.1 In the case of a patient detained under the Mental Health Act 1983 (MHA 1983), there are circumstances in which the nearest relative may:

- discharge the patient him- or herself or
- make an application to the Mental Health Review Tribunal in his or her own right.

The nearest relative's own power of discharge

7.2 The nearest relative has the power to make an order discharging a patient from detention or from guardianship under MHA 1983.[1] No discharge power exists where the patient is subject to supervised discharge. Where the patient is a ward of court, the nearest relative may only discharge him or her with the permission of the court.[2]

7.3 A similar power of discharge is possessed by (a) the patient's Responsible Medical Officer (RMO), (b) the managers (where the patient is detained in hospital), and (c) the relevant local social services authority (where the patient is

---

1   MHA 1983, s 23(1). See: Jones 2006, paras. 1–257 to 1–266; Department of Health and Welsh Office, *Mental Health Act 1983 Code of Practice*, 1999 [MHA 1983,*Code of Practice*], Chapter 23; Department of Health, *Mental Health Act 1983: Memorandum on Parts I to VI, VIII and X*, 1995, HMSO [MHA 1983 *Memorandum*], paras. 102–105 and 106.
2   MHA 1983, s 33(2).

subject to guardianship). The discharge power of each person or body may be exercised without reference to the others.[3]

7.4 The discharge power applies in relation to a patient detained under section 2 or 3 (or even section 4) of MHA 1983. It also applies to patients whom a court has placed under a hospital order or a guardianship order under section 37. It even applies in the case of a patient who is the subject of a restriction order (but in those circumstances, a patient will not have a nearest relative, and the person who would otherwise have been the nearest relative will have no power to order discharge.[4])

7.5 Where a patient is in hospital, not under MHA 1983, but informally, there will be no need for him or her to be discharged from detention and the person who would be his or her nearest relative will have no power in that regard.

Discharge by the nearest relative

7.6 The nearest relative may make an order for discharge at any time during the patient's MHA 1983 detention or guardianship. The discharge order must be in writing, but there is nothing in the Act to specify the form it must take or, indeed, the grounds upon which it might be made.[5]

7.7 Where such an order is made by the nearest relative, a patient will be discharged 72 hours after notice of the order was served upon the hospital managers or the responsible social services authority.[6] (This will not be the case, and the patient will remain liable to be detained, if, within the 72-hour period, the patient's RMO makes a 'barring report'.[7])

7.8 Although an order for discharge by the nearest relative need not be in a particular form, it may be:

- in *Form 34*, where the patient is detained in hospital[8] or

- in *Form 35*, where the patient is subject to guardianship.[9]

7.9 In fact, the MHA 1983 Code of Practice suggests that the managers of a hospital should ensure that a suitable form is available on which the nearest relative might make his or her order for discharge.[10]

---

3   MHA 1983 *Memorandum*, para. 102.
4   MHA 1983, Sched 1, Pt I, paras. 2 and 8 and Pt II, paras. 2 and 7.
5   *R (Wirral Health Authority and Wirral Borough Council) v Dr Finnegan and DE* [2001] EWHC 312 (Admin).
6   MHA 1983 *Memorandum*, para. 105.
7   See paras. **7.21–7.27**.
8   Mental Health (Hospital, Guardianship and Consent to Treatment) Regulations 1983 [Regulations], reg 15(1).
9   *Ibid.*, reg 15(2).
10   MHA 1983 *Code of Practice*, para. 22.10.

7.10 An order for discharge by the nearest relative must be served upon:

- the managers, if the patient is liable to be detained in hospital[11] or
- the responsible social services authority, if the patient is subject to guardianship.[12]

7.11 Where the order is for a patient's discharge from detention, or from liability to be detained, in hospital, it must be served:

- by delivering it at the hospital in question to an officer whom the managers have authorised to receive it or
- by sending it by prepaid post to the managers at the hospital.[13]

7.12 The managers in the case of a patient liable to be detained in hospital will be:

- *where it is a NHS hospital,* the NHS primary care trust, hospital trust, care trust, NHS foundation trust, strategic health authority, health authority or special health authority in which the hospital is vested or
- *where it is an establishment registered under the Care Standards Act 2000,* the person(s), body or bodies registered in respect of that establishment.[14]

7.13 It has been suggested that: 'all hospitals in which patients are detained should have suitable arrangements for opening post, whether delivered by hand or by the Post Office, at weekends and during holidays. As soon as the notice [of discharge] is received, the time of receipt should be recorded and the [RMO] should be informed.'[15] Furthermore, the managers should ensure that suitable persons are authorised to receive documents, such as a notice from the nearest relative, discharging a patient from detention.[16] (The authority granted to such persons need not be in writing.[17])

7.14 In one case, the High Court held that a nearest relative had not properly served a discharge order where it had simply been handed to a ward receptionist, who was not authorised to receive such a document on behalf of the managers. The court held that the order had in fact been received by the managers several days later, when it first came into the hands of the Mental Health Act administrator, and that a failure to provide a 'barring certificate' in the interim would not prevent the RMO from doing so at that point.[18]

---

11   Regulations, reg 15(1).
12   *Ibid.,* reg 15(2).
13   *Ibid.,* reg 3(3).
14   MHA 1983, s 145(1).
15   MHA 1983 *Memorandum,* para. 105.
16   *Ibid.,* para. 59.
17   Regulations, reg 3(3).
18   *Re G K (Patient: Habeas Corpus)* [1999] MHLR 128.

7.15 Where the order is for a patient's discharge from guardianship, it may be served:

- by delivering it to the relevant social services authority
- upon any person whom that authority has authorised to receive it[19]
- by sending it by prepaid post addressed to the authority at its registered or principal office or
- in the case of an individual authorised by the authority to receive it, at his or her usual or last known residence.[20]

7.16 Where a patient is subject to guardianship, the responsible local social services authority will be:

- the local social services authority that is his or her guardian[21] or
- if he or she has a private guardian, the local social services authority for the area in which that private guardian resides.[22]

Advising the nearest relative

7.17 If a nearest relative requires expert advice as to whether he or she should exercise the discharge power, he or she may appoint a registered medical practitioner to provide it. If so appointed, that practitioner may (a) visit the patient, (b) examine him or her in private and (c) require the production of, or inspect, any records relating to his or her detention or treatment, or to the aftercare services provided to the patient under section 117.[23]

7.18 The nearest relative who is considering discharging a patient would do well to seek such advice. The Court of Appeal has said:

> Any sensible nearest relative who was unhappy about the decisions made by the professionals would wish to seek such advice rather than rush to discharge the patient, thus placing at possible risk not only the patient's welfare but also her own status as nearest relative.[24]

7.19 In the context of guardianship, however, there are two 'obvious gaps' in the powers of the independent adviser:

---

19   Regulations, reg 3(1)(a).
20   *Ibid.*, reg 3(1)(b).
21   MHA 1983, s 34(3)(a).
22   MHA 1983, s 34(3)(b).
23   MHA 1983, s 24(2). See Jones 2006, paras. 1–267 to 1–274.
24   *R (Stevens) v Plymouth City Council and another* [2002] EWCA Civ 388, *per* Hale LJ at [22].

- they only enable a *doctor* to visit the patient and examine his or her records, whereas in guardianship cases often a *social worker* is best placed to undertake those tasks and

- they provide for the disclosure only of hospital and aftercare records, and give no right to examine social services records.[25]

7.20 These deficiencies, and what it saw as the need to rectify them, persuaded the Court of Appeal to grant general disclosure to the nearest relative of a patient who was subject to guardianship.[26]

Barring discharge by the nearest relative

7.21 In response to a nearest relative's notice of discharge, the patient's RMO may furnish to the managers a report 'certifying that in the opinion of [the RMO] the patient, if discharged, would be likely to act in a manner dangerous to other persons or to himself'.[27]

7.22 The RMO has no power to furnish a barring report in the case of a patient who is subject to guardianship. In such a case, an order made by the nearest relative would have the effect of discharging the patient from guardianship after 72 hours.

7.23 It has been said that the purpose of the 'barring report' 'is to ensure that the mere desire of, in particular, a closest relative to have a patient out does not defeat the purpose of the Act[,] which, both in the interests of the patient and the interests of the public, has ultimate regard to the patient's mental state'.[28]

7.24 As far as concerns 'dangerousness' within the meaning of MHA 1983, it has been held to connote: a 'very high level of probability that lasting psychological harm could be caused to others if the barring order were to be lifted'.[29]

7.25 Any barring report by the RMO *must* be in Part I of *Form 36* (and the receipt of the barring report by the managers *must* be in Part II of *Form 36*).[30]

7.26 If the RMO furnishes such a report within 72 hours following the receipt by the managers of the nearest relative's notice of discharge:

- that notice will be of no effect[31]

25   *Ibid.*
26   *Ibid.*, per Hale LJ at [40].
27   MHA 1983, s 25(1). See: Jones 2006, paras. 1–274 to 1–282; MHA 1093 *Memorandum*, paras. 102–106.
28   *Gary Kinsey v North Mersey Community NHS Trust*, Divisional Court, 21 June 1999, *per* Sedley LJ.
29   *Re Whitbread* [1999] COD 370. See further Jones 2006, para. 1–277.
30   Regulations, reg 15(3).
31   MHA 1983, s 25(1)(a).

- the nearest relative may not make a further order for the patient's discharge within a period of six months beginning with the date of his or her notice[32] and

- where the patient is detained under section 3 of MHA 1983, the managers must inform the nearest relative of the barring report furnished by the RMO.[33] (In such circumstances, the nearest relative will have the right to apply to a Mental Health Review Tribunal.[34] The nearest relative of a patient detained under section 2 has no such right.)

7.27 It is not clear when a nearest relative who intends to discharge a patient is deemed to have given notice to that effect.[35] However, the following is the likeliest (and possibly the most appropriate) sequence.

- When the nearest relative first delivers a written document, intimating his or her intention that the patient be discharged, he or she thereby gives notice to that effect under section 25(1) of MHA 1983.

- The notice will take effect 72 hours later, unless it is barred by a report furnished by the RMO.

- The nearest relative is at liberty to withdraw his or her notice within that 72-hour period, at least until the RMO furnishes his or her barring report.

- If the nearest relative *does* withdraw the notice before discharge is barred by the RMO, the nearest relative will retain the right to make a fresh order for the patient's discharge at any time during his or her period of detention, and even within the ensuing six months.

- Once the RMO has furnished a barring report, it is too late for the nearest relative to withdraw his or her notice of discharge.

Review by the managers

7.28 Where the RMO furnishes them with a barring report, the managers must consider holding a review of the patient's detention.[36] (In strict terms, the only requirement is that they *consider* doing so, not that they actually hold such a review.)

---

32   MHA 1983, s 25(1)(b).
33   MHA 1983, s 25(2).
34   See para. **7.41** *et seq.*
35   See, for example, Jones 2006, para. 1–276.
36   MHA 1983 *Code of Practice*, para. 23.8b.

7.29 The purpose of any such review by the managers would be to decide whether they should utilise their power to discharge the patient from detention under MHA 1983.

7.30 The managers' power of discharge may be exercised by any three or more members of a committee or subcommittee set up for the purpose.[37] This means that:

- where, as is usual, the committee (or subcommittee) has three members, they must be unanimous if the patient is to be discharged (and if they are not unanimous, the patient will remain liable to detention)

- if the committee (or subcommittee) has fewer than three members, it cannot lawfully discharge the patient and

- if the committee (or subcommittee) has more than three members, a simple majority of them will suffice for a patient to be discharged.

7.31 When conducting such a review, the managers must discharge the patient unless they are satisfied that all of the following criteria are met.

1. The patient is still suffering from mental disorder.

2. The patient's mental disorder is of a nature or degree that makes treatment in hospital appropriate.

3. Detention in hospital is still necessary in the interests of the patient's health or safety, or for the protection of other people.[38]

4. The patient, if discharged, would be likely to act in a manner dangerous to other persons or to him- or herself.[39]

7.32 This final criterion 'focuses on the probability of dangerous acts, such as causing serious physical injury, [and] not merely the patient's general need for safety and others' general need for protection: it provides a more stringent test for continuing detention'.[40] If the managers fail to apply it and decide not to discharge the patient, their decision will be irrational and may be quashed.[41]

7.33 Even if the managers apply the final criterion, they are entitled to come to a different conclusion than the RMO on the question of the patient's 'dangerousness'. This will not, however, lead to their being *required* to discharge the patient,

37   *R (Tagoe-Thompson) v The Hospital Managers of the Park Royal Centre* [2003] EWCA Civ 330.
38   MHA 1983 *Code of Practice*, para. 23.11.
39   *R v Riverside Mental Health Trust, ex parte Huzzey* (1998) 43 BMLR 167. See also MHA 1983 *Code of Practice*, para. 23.12.
40   MHA 1983 *Code of Practice*, para. 23.12.
41   *R v Riverside Mental Health Trust, ex parte Huzzey* (1998) 43 BMLR 167.

for they have a residual discretion *not* to order discharge, even in those circumstances.[42]

Mental Health Review Tribunals

7.34 The Mental Health Review Tribunal (MHRT) has the power to discharge a patient from (a) detention, (b) guardianship or (c) supervised discharge under MHA 1983. (In some circumstances, it may also make recommendations about a MHA 1983 patient's care and treatment, but that power is not discussed further here.)[43]

7.35 A patient may personally apply to the MHRT.[44]

7.36 There are some circumstances in which the nearest relative of a patient will also have the right to apply to a MHRT. In order for the nearest relative to enjoy such a right, the patient will have to be:

1. liable to be detained under section 2, 3 or 4 of MHA 1983

2. subject to guardianship under section 7

3. subject to supervised discharged under section 25A-J[45] or

4. the subject of a hospital order or a guardianship order made under section 37.[46]

7.37 Where the patient is a ward of court, the nearest relative may only apply to the MHRT with the permission of the court.[47]

7.38 Although a patient whose hospital order or guardianship order has been combined with a restriction order[48] may apply to a MHRT, that patient will not, of course, have a nearest relative, and the person who would otherwise have been his or her nearest relative will have no power to make a tribunal application.[49]

7.39 Where the right to apply to the MHRT exists in relation to a patient whose nearest relative has been displaced by the court, it will be exercisable by the *acting* nearest relative, not by the *displaced* nearest relative. However, the displaced nearest relative will have the right to make one application to the MHRT in the 12 months after the date of the order displacing him or her, and, for as long as the

---

42   *R (SR) v Huntercombe Maidenhead Hospital* [2005] EWHC 2361 (Admin), *per* Jackson J at [19]
43   See Jones 2006, paras. 1–755 to 1–876. See also: MHA 1983 *Memorandum,* paras. 231–259. Helpful guidance, together with specimen forms, may be obtained from the MHRT website, at www.mhrt.org.uk. See also: Gostin 1986, Chapter 18; Gostin and Fennell 1992; Eldergill 1997.
44   See, for example, MHA 1983, ss 66, 69 and 70.
45   MHA 1983, s 66(1) and (2).
46   MHA 1983, Sch 1, Pt I, paras. 2 and 9.
47   MHA 1983, s 33(2).
48   Made under ss 41 or 49 of MHA 1983.
49   MHA 1983, s 70.

patient remains subject to MHA 1983, one further such application in each succeeding 12-month period.[50]

7.40 The purpose of an application to the MHRT (including one by a nearest relative) will be to secure an order discharging the patient from liability to be detained, from guardianship, or from supervised discharge under MHA 1983.

The right to apply

7.41 In the case of a patient who is subject to the civil provisions in MHA 1983 – namely, sections 2, 3, 4 or 7 – his or her nearest relative may apply to the MHRT where:

- a report is furnished to the managers by the RMO under section 16 of MHA 1983, the effect of which is to reclassify the patient[51]
- a supervision application is accepted in respect of the patient[52]
- a report is furnished under section 25F of MHA 1983 in respect of the patient, the effect of which is to re-classify the patient while he or she is subject to supervised discharge[53]
- a report is furnished under section 25G of MHA 1983 in respect of the patient, the effect of which is to renew his or her supervised discharge.[54]

7.42 A nearest relative may apply to the MHRT, provided (a) he or she was informed of these events or (b) he or she was *entitled* to be so informed.[55] This means, for example, that:

- If the patient objected to the nearest relative's being informed of the event in question and there were grounds on which the objection could be respected, the nearest relative will have been neither (a) informed nor (b) entitled to be informed of that event, and he or she will not be able to apply to the MHRT because of it.
- Where, even though there was no objection from the patient, the nearest relative was not informed of the event in question (even though steps that appeared to be practicable were taken in that regard), he or

50 MHA 1983, s 66(2)(g).
51 MHA 1983, s 66(1)(i).
52 *Ibid.*
53 *Ibid.*
54 *Ibid.*
55 *Ibid.*

she will still be entitled to apply to the MHRT because of that event when – and however – he or she subsequently comes to find out about it.

7.43 If the nearest relative makes application to the MHRT on any of these grounds, he or she will do so to the exclusion of the patient: the right is for one or other of them – and not for *both* of them – to make the application.

7.44 There are also circumstances in which the nearest relative of a civil patient will have a less limited right to apply to the MHRT. They are where:

- a report is furnished to the managers by the RMO under section 25 of MHA 1983, the effect of which is to bar an order for the patient's discharge made by the nearest relative under section 23[56]

- a patient is liable to be detained under a hospital order (provided not less than six months have elapsed since the patient became so subject)[57]

- a patient is subject to a guardianship order (at any time during the currency of that order)[58] or

- an order is made under section 29 of MHA 1983, effectively displacing the nearest relative of a patient, and the patient is, or subsequently comes to be, detained under MHA 1983. (The applicant in this case will be the acting nearest relative, not the displaced nearest relative.)[59]

7.45 The fact that the nearest relative has exercised his or her right under these grounds will not affect any right the patient has to apply to the MHRT personally.

7.46 Where the patient is a ward of court, the nearest relative will need the permission of the High Court to make an application to the MHRT.[60]

7.47 A nearest relative (or, indeed, any other person so entitled) may only make application to the MHRT at the times and in the circumstances specified in MHA 1983.[61] Thus, there is no power for a nearest relative to apply to the MHRT simply because:

- the patient has been detained under section 2 or section 3 of MHA 1983, or made subject to guardianship

- a patient is transferred from guardianship to hospital or

---

56   MHA 1983, s 66(1)(ii). As to the nearest relative's right to order a patient's discharge, see paras. **7.6–7.16**; as to the RMO's power to bar such an order, see paras. **7.21–7.27**.
57   MHA 1983, s 69(1)(a).
58   *Ibid.*
59   MHA 1983, s 66(1)(ii). As to the process by which a nearest relative might be displaced, see para. **4.23** et seq.
60   MHA 1983, s 33(2).
61   MHA 1983, s 77(1) and (2).

- a patient's liability to detention (as opposed to supervised discharge) is renewed.

Time limits

7.48 Where a patient has been re-classified, either (a) under section 16 of MHA 1983, while liable to be detained, or (b) under section 25F, while subject to supervised discharge, any application by the nearest relative must be made to the MHRT within 28 days of the day on which he or she is informed that the relevant report has been furnished.[62]

7.49 Where a patient is made the subject of a supervision application, any application by the nearest relative must be made to the MHRT within six months of the day on which the application is accepted.[63] (Where he or she has been consulted about a supervision application, the nearest relative has the right to be informed when it is made.[64] But since there is nothing to state *when* the nearest relative should be informed, it is possible that the time within which he or she might make any application to the MHRT will be reduced to something considerably less than six months.)

7.50 Where a report is furnished under section 25G of MHA 1983, the effect of which is to renew a patient's supervised discharge, any application by the nearest relative may be made to the MHRT at any time within the further period during which the patient is subject to supervised discharge.[65]

7.51 Where a report is furnished under section 25 of MHA 1983, the effect of which is to bar an order for the patient's discharge made by the nearest relative under section 23, any application by the nearest relative must be made to the MHRT within 28 days of the day on which he or she is informed that the relevant report has been furnished.[66]

7.52 Where an order is made under section 29 of MHA 1983, effectively displacing the nearest relative of a patient, and the patient is, or subsequently comes to be, detained under MHA 1983, an application by the nearest relative may be made to the MHRT (a) at any time within a period of 12 months beginning with the date of the order, and (b) in any subsequent period of 12 months during which the order continues in force.[67]

---

62   MHA 1983, s 66(2)(d).
63   MHA 1983, s 66(2)(c).
64   MHA 1983, ss 25A(8)(c) and 25B(2)(b).
65   MHA 1983, s 66(2)(fa).
66   MHA 1983, s 66(2)(d).
67   MHA 1983, s 66(2)(g).

7.53 Where a patient is the subject of a hospital order, the nearest relative may apply to the MHRT (a) once in the first 12-month period after the order was made (but only in the second six months of that period), and (b) once in any subsequent period of 12 months during which the patient remains subject to the order.[68]

7.54 Where a patient is the subject of a guardianship order, the nearest relative may apply to the MHRT (a) once in the first 12 months after the order was made, and (b) once in any subsequent period of 12 months during which the patient remains subject to the order.[69]

Making the application

7.55 This section discusses the steps a nearest relative will have to take in order to apply to the MHRT, and the processes in which he or she might expect to become involved by doing so.

WHICH TRIBUNAL?

7.56 There are three MHRT offices, which cover:

1. the southern region of England, comprising Gloucestershire, Oxfordshire, Buckinghamshire, Hertfordshire, Essex and all counties south and south-west of them

2. the northern region of England, which comprises all the other counties of England

3. Wales.

7.57 An application to the MHRT, including one by a patient's nearest relative, should be made as follows:

- where the patient is liable to be detained in hospital, to the MHRT office for the area in which the hospital is situated

- where the patient is subject to guardianship, to the MHRT office for the area in which he or she is residing

- where the patient is, or is to be, subject to supervised discharge, to the MHRT office for the area in which he or she is residing or is to reside.[70]

7.58 In fact, although each regional office has its own address, the address to which MHRT applications should be sent is the same in each case:

---

68   MHA 1983, s 69(1)(a).
69   MHA 1983, s 69(1)(b)(ii).
70   MHA 1983, s 77(3).

Mental Health Review Tribunal,
5th Floor
11 Belgrave Road
London SW1V 1RS

WHAT SHOULD THE APPLICATION CONTAIN?

7.59 The contents of an application to the MHRT are specified in the Mental Health Review Tribunal Rules 1983.[71]

7.60 An application by a nearest relative to the MHRT must:

- be in writing
- be signed by the nearest relative (or by someone he or she has authorised to do so).[72]

7.61 There is no particular format for a MHRT application, although the tribunal has produced specimen forms that, if completed, would contain all the required information. Those forms are available at
www.mhrt.org.uk/resources/forms_leaflets/applications_forms.htm

7.62 Wherever possible, a MHRT application by a nearest relative should contain the following information:

- the name of the patient[73]
- the patient's address, including (as appropriate), that of the place where he or she is detained, or that of any private guardian[74]
- the name and address of the nearest relative-applicant and his or her relationship to the patient[75]
- the section of MHA 1983 to which the patient is subject[76]
- the name and address of any representative for the nearest relative-applicant that has been authorised under Rule 10. This might be a solicitor, barrister or legal executive, or it might simply be a relative or friend. (Where no such representative has yet been authorised, the nearest relative-applicant should state whether he or she intends to authorise a representative or wishes to conduct his or her own case.)[77]

---

71   SI 1983 No 942.
72   Mental Health Review Tribunal Rules 1983 [MHRT Rules], r 3(1).
73   MHRT Rules, r 3(2)(a).
74   MHRT Rules, r 3(2)(b).
75   MHRT Rules, r 3(2)(c).
76   MHRT Rules, r 3(2)(d).
77   MHRT Rules, r 3(2)(e).

7.63 Because the requirement is simply to provide this information 'wherever possible', failure to provide it will not invalidate an application.

SUPERVISED DISCHARGE

7.64 If the patient is – or is to be – subject to supervised discharge, any application to the MHRT (for example by the nearest relative) must also include:

- the names of the patient's community RMO and supervisor[78]

- the name and address of any place at which the patient is to receive medical treatment[79]

- the patient's current address.[80]

The response to an application

7.65 Where a patient is detained under section 2 of MHA 1983, the nearest relative may not, of course, make an application to the MHRT in his or her own right. If such is practicable, however, the nearest relative will be entitled to receive notice of any such application (and ultimately, of the date, time and place fixed for the hearing).[81]

7.66 Where an application is made to the MHRT (for example, by the nearest relative of a patient), those who are detaining the patient, or are responsible for his or her guardianship, will have to send to the MHRT:

- a statement that includes, among other things, the name and address of the nearest relative[82]

- an up-to-date social circumstances report, which will include, among other things, the attitude of the patient's nearest relative.[83] (This suggests that those views will have to be canvassed in preparation for the MHRT hearing.)

7.67 When it receives the statement of the relevant authority, the MHRT must:

- send a copy of it to the nearest relative (if he or she is the applicant)[84]

- give notice of the proceedings to the nearest relative (*unless* he or she is the applicant).[85] (In a case concerning a restricted patient, no such

---

78   MHRT Rules, r 3(2)(f)(i).
79   MHRT Rules, r 3(2)(f)(ii).
80   MHRT Rules, r 3(2)(f)(iii).
81   MHRT Rules, r 31(c).
82   MHRT Rules, r 6(1), and Sch 1, Pt A, cl 11 and Pt E, cl 12.
83   MHRT Rules, r 6(1), and Sch 1, Pt B, cl 2(a) and Pt F, cl 2(a) or 3(a).
84   MHRT Rules, r 6(5).
85   MHRT Rules, r 7(d).

notice need or should be given to the person who, were the patient not subject to restrictions, would be his or her nearest relative.)

7.68 The MHRT may decide to withhold from the applicant (including a nearest relative-applicant) a copy of the statement of the detaining authority, if it believes that disclosure of the statement would adversely affect the health or welfare of the patient or others.[86]

7.69 Where the nearest relative is the applicant, the MHRT must, as soon as practicable, send him or her a copy of every document it receives that is relevant to the application.[87]

7.70 The MHRT may withhold from the applicant (including a nearest relative-applicant) any document it has received that is relevant to an application but whose disclosure would adversely affect the health or welfare of the patient or others.[88]

7.71 But even if a MHRT withholds a document from an applicant (including a nearest relative-applicant), it must disclose that document to any representative of his or hers who is:

1. a barrister

2. a registered medical practitioner

3. in the opinion of the MHRT, a suitable person by virtue of his or her experience or professional qualifications.[89]

7.72 Where such a person has information disclosed to him or her in these circumstances, he or she may not:

1. disclose it to the applicant (including a nearest relative-applicant) or the patient without the permission of the MHRT or

2. use the information otherwise than in connection with the application.[90]

The hearing

7.73 An applicant (including a nearest relative-applicant) must be given at least 14 days' notice of the date, time and place fixed for a MHRT hearing.[91]

---

86   MHRT Rules, r 6(4)(b).
87   MHRT Rules, r 12(1).
88   MHRT Rules, r 12(2).
89   MHRT Rules, r 12(3).
90   *Ibid.*
91   MHRT Rules, r 20.

7.74 Where a patient is detained under section 2 of MHA 1983, the nearest relative may not make an application to the MHRT in his or her own right. If such was practicable, however, the nearest relative will have received notice of any such application, and will be given the date, time and place fixed for the hearing.[92]

7.75 Where he or she is the applicant, the nearest relative will be able to appear at a MHRT hearing and take such part in the proceedings as the tribunal thinks proper.[93] (Even if he or she is not the applicant, the nearest relative may do this, but only with the permission of the MHRT.)

7.76 An applicant (including a nearest relative-applicant) must be heard and his or her evidence taken by the MHRT, and he or she will be entitled to hear the evidence of other witnesses, call his or her own witnesses, and put questions to them all.[94]

7.77 Where he or she is the applicant, the nearest relative will be given the opportunity to address the MHRT once all the evidence has been given.[95]

7.78 These rights are subject to Rule 21(4), which provides that the MHRT may exclude from any hearing or part of a hearing any person or class of persons. If it uses this power to exclude an applicant (including a nearest relative-applicant):

1.   the MHRT must inform him or her of its reasons and record those reasons in writing and

2.   it may not exclude his or her representative from the hearing.

7.79 The decision of a MHRT, including one in respect of an application made by a nearest relative, may be announced at the end of a hearing. In any case, the decision will be communicated in writing to the parties – including, if appropriate, a nearest relative-applicant – within seven days.[96]

7.80 When communicating its decision to anyone apart from the patient, a MHRT may make such conditions as it considers appropriate concerning the disclosure of that decision to a patient.[97]

7.81 Where, however, the applicant (including a nearest relative-applicant) was *represented* at a hearing, the MHRT must disclose the full, recorded grounds of that decision to the representative (although, again, it may make conditions as to the disclosure of those grounds to the patient).[98]

---

92   MHRT Rules, r 31(c).
93   MHRT Rules, r 22(4).
94   *Ibid.*
95   MHRT Rules, r 22(5).
96   MHRT Rules, r 24(1).
97   MHRT Rules, r 24(2).
98   *Ibid.*

8

The Nearest Relative
and the Mental Capacity Act

This chapter compares the role of nearest relative with that of independent mental capacity advocate, and asks whether the two might in some circumstances converge.

Introduction

8.1 There is at least one role that might resemble that of the nearest relative under the Mental Health Act 1983 (MHA 1983). It arises under, and relates solely to, the Mental Capacity Act 2005 (MCA 2005). The role is that of the independent mental capacity advocate (IMCA).

8.2 The MCA 2005 also gives rights, or roles, to others that might, in one way or another, resemble the nearest relative. They are:

- a donee under a lasting power of attorney[1]
- a deputy appointed by the Court of Protection[2]
- someone named for the purpose by a person lacking capacity[3]
- someone who provides care to such a person[4]
- anyone else interested in the welfare of such a person.[5]

8.3 In time, a further role might be introduced that resembles that of the nearest relative. It is the representative of a person subject to the '*Bournewood* safeguards'.

---

1   See paras. **8.33** and **8.34**.
2   See paras. **8.35** and **8.36**.
3   See paras. **8.37–8.39**.
4   See paras. **8.40–8.46**.
5   See paras. **8.47** and **8.48**.

8.4 The MCA 2005 has received the Royal Assent, and much of it will come into effect in October 2007.[6] However, the provisions in the Act dealing with the appointment of independent mental capacity advocates came into force on 1 November 2006,[7] and the ones relating to the functions of such advocates and the circumstances in which they will be available came into force on 1 April 2007.[8] That is why those provisions are described here.

8.5 Although the *Bournewood* safeguards will be incorporated into MCA 2005, they are contained, not in that Act, but in the Mental Health Bill 2006, and they will therefore come into force only when (and if) that Bill has completed its passage through Parliament and the amendments it makes to the Mental Health Act 1983 have become law. Because this is not likely to be before 2008, the position of representatives appointed for so-called '*Bournewood* patients' is not considered here.[9]

8.6 The MCA 2005 provides a framework within which decisions might be taken on behalf of, and care and treatment provided to, people who lack capacity.[10] (MCA 2005 does not apply in the case of someone who is capable, even if he or she is suffering from 'mental disorder' within the meaning of MHA 1983.)

8.7 Where a patient is both lacking capacity within the meaning of MCA 2005 and suffering from mental disorder within the meaning of MHA 1983, it is possible that he or she will fall within both Acts.

The Mental Health Act and the Mental Capacity Act

8.8 In general terms, MHA 1983 trumps MCA 2005. That is to say: where a patient is liable to be detained under MHA 1983, the treatment he or she receives for his or her mental disorder will be given under that Act, and MCA 2005 will have no application. This means, for example, that the patient may be given that treatment – and, if necessary, compelled to have it – regardless of the wishes of any deputy he or she might have, or of a donee under any Lasting Power of Attorney (LPA) he or she might have created.[11]

---

6   See: Statement by the Parliamentary Under-Secretary of State, Department for Constitutional Affairs, 18 December 2006, Hansard, col WS230.

7   The Mental Capacity Act 2005 (Commencement No 1) Order 2006, SI 2006 No 2814, Article 5(a). See also: MCA 2005, s 35; The Mental Capacity Act 2005 (Independent Mental Capacity Advocates) (General) Regulations 2006 [IMCA (General) Regulations], SI 2006 No 1832.

8   The Mental Capacity Act 2005 (Commencement No 1) Order 2006, SI 2006 No 2814, Article 5(b). See also: MCA 2005, ss 36–41; The Mental Capacity Act 2005 (Independent Mental Capacity Advocates) (General) Regulations 2006, SI 2006 No 1832; The Mental Capacity Act 2005 (Independent Mental Capacity Advocates) (Expansion of Role) Regulations 2006, SI 2006 No 2883.

9   But see: Department of Health and Home Office, *Mental Health Bill*, November 2006, HL Bill 1 54/2, cl 38 and Scheds 6, 7 and 8. See also *ibid., Explanatory* Notes, nn 155–195.

10   For the MCA 2005, and for discussion of its provisions and implications, see: Ashton *et al.* 2006; Bartlett 2005, Greaney *et al.* 2005; Jones 2005.

11   MCA 2005, s 28(1).

8.9 MCA 2005 might, however, be relevant in the case of a patient liable to be detained under MHA 1983, but only if, as well as treatment for his or her mental disorder, that patient is also to receive general medical treatment. It is to that general treatment that MCA 2005 will apply.

8.10 Where, in the case of a patient who lacks capacity, he or she is not liable to be detained under MHA 1983, all of the patient's health care (and social care) will fall to be provided under MCA 2005, including treatment provided for any mental disorder from which he or she is suffering. This will be so whether the patient has been admitted to hospital or is to be treated at home.

The independent mental capacity advocate

8.11 One of the key elements of MCA 2005, and what makes it unique as a piece of legislation, is the Independent Mental Capacity Advocate Service and the statutory right the Act gives to some patients to access that service. The powers and duties of an independent mental capacity advocate (IMCA) are discussed elsewhere.[12]

8.12 The circumstances in which an incapable person will be entitled to the services of an IMCA are as follows:

- where 'serious medical treatment' is to be provided to him or her by the NHS[13]

- where the NHS arranges or changes the patient's accommodation in a hospital or care home, if that accommodation has lasted, or is likely to last, for more than 28 days (in a hospital) or eight weeks (in a care home)[14]

- where a local authority arranges or changes the patient's accommodation in residential accommodation, if that accommodation is of a certain kind and has lasted, or is likely to last, for more than eight weeks.[15]

8.13 Even in these circumstances, the patient will only be entitled to an IMCA where there is no one else, such as a donee, a deputy or an informal carer, whom it would be appropriate to consult about the patient's best interests.[16]

---

12   MCA 2005, ss 35–41. See, in particular, Greaney *et al*. 2005, Chapter 9.
13   MCA 2005, s 37(1)(a). See Appendix 1.
14   MCA 2005, s 38(1) and (3)-(5). See: Appendix 1; paras. **8.17–8.19**.
15   MCA 2005, s 39(1), (4) and (5). See: Appendix 1; paras. **8.17–8.19**.
16   MCA 2005, ss 37(1)(b), 38(2), 39(3) and 40. See Appendix 1.

8.14 Where, under MCA 2005, a person is entitled to the services of an IMCA, it will be the responsibility of the relevant NHS body or local authority to instruct one to represent him or her.[17]

Serious medical treatment

8.15 Under MCA 2005, 'serious medical treatment' means providing, withdrawing or withholding treatment in circumstances where –

- in a case where a single treatment is being proposed, there is a fine balance between its benefits to the patient and the burdens and risks it is likely to entail for him or her
- in a case where there is a choice of treatments, a decision as to which one to use is finely balanced
- what is proposed would be likely to involve serious consequences for the patient.[18]

8.16 This provision does not apply – and an incapable person will not be entitled to an IMCA – in so far as his or her treatment is regulated by the 'consent to treatment' provisions in Part IV of MHA 1983.[19] However, if the patient, as well as being subject to MHA 1983, is receiving treatment for something other than a mental disorder, he or she may be entitled to an IMCA if that treatment is 'serious medical treatment'.

Accommodation

8.17 Even though an incapable person might be accommodated in a hospital or care home, he or she will not be entitled to an IMCA if so accommodated as the result of an obligation imposed on him or her under MHA 1983.[20] This is so, whether the accommodation in question was arranged by the NHS or by a local authority. This means, for example, that an incapable person will not be entitled to the services of an IMCA solely because he or she is subject to guardianship.

8.18 In the case of residential accommodation provided by a local authority, there is an additional requirement: an IMCA will only be available if the accommodation is to be provided under (a) section 21 or 29 of the National Assistance Act 1948 or (b) section 117 of MHA 1983, and, if in either case, (c) such is the result of a

---

17   MCA 2005, ss 37(3), 38(3) and 39(4).
18   MCA 2005, s 37(6); IMCA (General) Regulations, reg 4(2).
19   MCA 2005, s 37(2).
20   MCA 2005, ss 38(2) and 39(3).

decision taken by the local authority under section 47 of the NHS and Community Care Act 1990.[21]

8.19 In summary, therefore, an incapable person who is also subject to MHA 1983 will not be entitled to an IMCA where:

- all of the treatment the patient receives falls within Part IV of MHA 1983 or

- the patient's accommodation – arranging of which would otherwise entitle him or her to the services of an IMCA – was arranged as a result of an obligation imposed upon the patient under MHA 1983. This will be so where, for example, the patient is (a) liable to be detained under section 3 or 37, or (b) subject to guardianship under section 7.

The IMCA

8.20 In order to be appointed in respect of a particular incapable person, an IMCA will have to:

- be approved by a local authority on the grounds that he or she satisfies the appointment requirements[22] or

- belong to a class of persons which itself is so approved.[23]

8.21 The appointment requirements for an IMCA are as follows:

- he or she must have appropriate experience and training

- he or she must be of integrity and good character

- he or she must be able to act independently of anyone who instructs him or her.[24]

8.22 Before deciding whether a person is of integrity and good character sufficient to be appointed an IMCA, the relevant local authority must obtain a criminal record certificate.[25]

8.23 As far as obtaining information is concerned, the functions of an IMCA are as follows:[26]

- to verify that his or her instructions were issued by someone authorised to give them

---

21 MCA 2005, s 39(2).
22 As to which, see para. **8.21**.
23 MCA 2005, s 35(3); IMCA (General) Regulations, reg 5(1).
24 MCA 2005, s 35(4); IMCA (General) Regulations, reg 5(2).
25 IMCA (General) Regulations, reg 5(3)(a) and (b); Police Act 1997, ss 113A and 113B.
26 MCA 2005, s 36; IMCA (General) Regulations, reg 6(4). See Appendix 1.

- to interview the patient in private[27]
- to examine and copy: (a) any health record; (b) any record made or held by a local authority and compiled in connection with a social services function; and/or (c) any record held by a person registered under Part 2 of the Care Standards Act 2000.[28] (However, access may be gained to these documents only if the person holding them considers that they may be relevant to the IMCA's investigation. The decision, it would seem, is not for the IMCA to make.)
- in so far as it is practicable and appropriate to do so, to consult: (a) anyone providing care for the patient in a professional capacity or for remuneration; or (b) anyone else who might be able to comment on the patient's wishes, feelings, beliefs or values
- to take all practicable steps to obtain such other information as the IMCA considers necessary.[29]

8.24 Once the information is to hand, the IMCA must evaluate it so as to ascertain:

- the extent of the support provided to the patient to enable him or her to participate in making any decision about the matter in relation to which the IMCA has been instructed
- the patient's wishes and feelings, and the beliefs and values that would be likely to influence him or her, if he or she were capable
- the alternative courses of action available for the patient
- where medical treatment is proposed for the patient, whether he or she might benefit from a further medical opinion.[30]

The IMCA and the nearest relative

8.25 As we have seen,[31] where the arrangements made are for an incapable person to be accommodated because he or she is subject to MHA 1983, those arrangements will not entitle him or her to an IMCA. This is so whether the arrangements are made by the NHS or by a local authority. For that reason, it is only where the person is to be provided with serious medical treatment by the NHS that an IMCA might come into contact with a nearest relative.

---

27   MHA 1983, s 35(6)(a).
28   MHA 1983, s 35(6)(b).
29   MCA 2005, s 36; IMCA (General) Regulations, reg 6(4). See Appendix 1.
30   MCA 2005, s 36(2); IMCA (General) Regulations, reg 6(5).
31   See para. **8.17**.

8.26 Where the 'serious medical treatment' concerned is entirely covered by Part IV of the MHA 1983, no IMCA will be required.[32] Therefore, a person is only likely to have *both* an IMCA *and* a nearest relative where he or she is incapable within the meaning of MCA 2005 and:

- he or she is liable to be detained under MHA 1983 and

- he or she is receiving (or is to receive) serious medical treatment in addition to any treatment for mental disorder.

8.27 In any such circumstances, the scope for conflict between the IMCA and the nearest relative would be very limited, because:

- the IMCA would have rights under the MCA 2005 to the exclusion of the nearest relative *but*

- only the nearest relative would have rights in respect of treatment provided to the patient under MHA 1983.

8.28 In the case of an *informal* patient admitted to hospital for treatment for mental disorder:

- if that treatment were to fulfil the definition of 'serious medical treatment' in MCA 2005, the patient would have to be provided with an IMCA *but*

- because he or she was not liable to be detained under MHA 1983, there would be no nearest relative who had a role to play.

8.29 In fact, the roles of nearest relative and of IMCA resemble each other: first, in that they will come into being in specified circumstances; but second, in that those circumstances – whether under MCA 2005 or MHA 1983 – do not encompass all interventions possible under those Acts.

8.30 The two roles are, however, different in a number of ways.

- The IMCA is the representative of last resort, but, where he or she has them, the nearest relative will enjoy his or her rights to the exclusion of all others.

- There are fairly strict criteria, at least for the initial appointment of an IMCA, with even the possibility of police checks. The same simply cannot be said of the nearest relative, whose powers, as we have seen and numerous cases demonstrate,[33] may devolve upon a person who is wholly unsuitable for the role. It is interesting, however, that despite their quite detailed requirements as to an IMCA's experience, training,

32   MCA 2005, s 37(2).
33   See paras. 1.15–1.21.

integrity, good character and independence, neither MCA 2005 nor the Regulations contains an express provision that could prohibit an IMCA from acting in a case whose specific circumstances make it inappropriate for him or her to do so.

- It is arguable that the functions of the IMCA are broader than those of the nearest relative. They encompass a variety of things that do not fall within the statutory ambit of the nearest relative. For example: (a) there is an unambiguous investigatory role for the IMCA that simply is not countenanced in MHA 1983; and (b) there is a right to the disclosure of documents that, while hardly unfettered, is a good deal more specific than anything available to the nearest relative.

- Seen in another light, however, the powers of the IMCA are more nebulous than those in MHA 1983: there is no equivalent, for example, of the nearest relative's power of discharge.[34] (This might reflect a basic conceptual difference between MCA 2005 and MHA 1983, with the latter possessing a keener coercive edge than any to be discerned in the former.)

- The differences in the circumstances that will bring about their appointment mean that even where an IMCA and a nearest relative find themselves acting in the case of the same patient, their roles will never overlap.

8.31 Where a patient subject to MHA 1983 is also entitled to the services of an IMCA, it is highly unlikely that the person appointed as his or her advocate will also be the nearest relative. (Although there is nothing that would expressly prohibit such a state of affairs, it is submitted that if it should arise, it would create the possibility of a conflict of interest.)

Other people

8.32 The MCA 2005 also makes reference to other people, who may not be the IMCA or the nearest relative of a person who lacks capacity, but who nevertheless have a number of rights and responsibilities in connection with him or her. Those people are:

- the donee under a lasting power of attorney
- a deputy appointed by the Court of Protection

---

34   See paras. **7.6–7.16**.

- someone named for the purpose by a person lacking capacity[35]
- someone who provides care to an incapable person[36] and
- anyone else interested in the welfare of an incapable person.[37]

The donee

8.33 The donee is the person to whom, when he or she was still capable, a person gave various powers under a LPA. The functions of a donee have been described elsewhere,[38] but in some circumstances, the donee might even have the power to require treatment to be withheld from the person who now lacks capacity.

8.34 It is possible that the person whom a patient appoints his or her donee under a LPA will also be his or her nearest relative within the meaning of the MHA 1983. Even if that is so, the donee's powers under MCA 2005 will not supplement those available to him or her as nearest relative. In particular, any power derived from the LPA to require that medical treatment be withheld from the patient will not apply where that treatment is to be given under MHA 1983. (This would also be the case if the donee was not also the patient's nearest relative under MHA 1983.)

The deputy

8.35 A deputy is the person appointed by the Court of Protection to act for, and make decisions on behalf of, a person lacking capacity. The functions of a deputy have been described elsewhere,[39] but in many circumstances they will include the power to consent to (or to withhold consent for) the providing of medical treatment to the person who lacks capacity.

8.36 Again, it is possible that the person whom the Court of Protection appoints as the deputy for an incapable person will also be the nearest relative within the meaning of the MHA 1983. Even if that is so, the deputy's powers under MCA 2005 will not supplement those available to him or her as nearest relative. In particular, any power to require that medical treatment be withheld from the patient will not apply where that treatment is to be given under MHA 1983. (This would also be the case if the deputy was not also the patient's nearest relative under MHA 1983.)

---

35   See paras. **8.37–8.39**.
36   See paras. **8.40–8.46**.
37   See paras. **8.47–8.48**.
38   See, for example: Ashton *et al.* 2006, Chapter 3; Bartlett 2005, paras. 2.65–2.82; Greaney *et al.* 2005, Chapter 4; Jones 2005, pp.35–42.
39   See, for example: Ashton *et al.* 2006, paras. 4.20–4.33; Bartlett 2005, paras. 2.83–2.100; Greaney *et al.* 2005, Chapter 6; Jones 2005, pp.49–52.

The person named

8.37 In the case of a person who lacks capacity, anyone he or she has named for the purpose has certain limited rights when a decision has to be made as to the incapable person's 'best interests'.[40] Such a person must be consulted, provided it is both 'practicable' and 'appropriate' to do so, and his or her views must be taken into account.[41] In particular, account must be taken of what the person named says about:

- the incapable person's own past and present wishes and feelings (which might have been set down in a written statement, made before the person became incapable)
- the beliefs and values that are likely to have influenced the incapable person if he or she had not become such and
- the other factors that the incapable person would be likely to consider if he or she were able to do so.[42]

8.38 The process by which the 'best interests' of an incapable person might be ascertained has been described elsewhere.[43]

8.39 The role of anyone named in this way will only be the one set out in MCA 2005: it will not convey any MHA 1983 rights, and the person concerned will only enjoy such rights if he or she acquires them by other means. If he or she also happens to be the patient's nearest relative, the person named will acquire no greater MHA 1983 rights by reason of having been so named.

The carer

8.40 Where a person lacks capacity, MCA 2005 gives certain rights to anyone who is providing care to him or her. Those rights relate to (a) the best interests of the incapable person and (b) any research that might be carried out on him or her.

---

40   As to which, see MCA 2005, s 4.
41   MCA 2005, s 4(7)(a).
42   MCA 2005, s 4(7)(a) and (6).
43   See, for example: Ashton *et al*. 2006, paras. 2.89–2.112; Bartlett 2005, paras. 2.31–2.48; Greaney *et al*. 2005, para. 3.4; Jones 2005, pp.20–26.

BEST INTERESTS

8.41 In the case of a person with incapacity, anyone engaged in caring for him or her has certain limited rights when a decision has to be made as to the incapable person's 'best interests'.[44] Those rights are equivalent to the ones possessed by anyone named by the incapable person in this regard.[45]

RESEARCH

8.42 A carer also has certain rights where it is proposed to carry out research on the person with incapacity.[46] (However, he or she will only have these rights if he or she provides care otherwise than in a professional capacity or for remuneration.[47])

8.43 The person carrying out the research must take 'reasonable steps' to identify a carer.[48] If that person is willing to be consulted,[49] the researcher must, first, provide him or her with information about the project and, second, ask him or her:

- whether the person with incapacity should take part in the project[50] and

- what, in the carer's opinion, the wishes and feelings of the person would have been if he or she had been capable.[51]

8.44 The researcher need not consult a carer where it is not reasonably practicable to do so, but only if urgent treatment is, or is to be, provided to the person without capacity as a matter of urgency, and even then, only if certain other circumstances also apply.[52]

8.45 If he or she had been capable, the person without capacity might have refused to take part in the research project. If the person engaged in providing care tells the researcher that the person would indeed have refused, the person without capacity must not take part (or any further part) in the project.[53]

8.46 The process by which the views of an incapable person upon his or her participation in a research project might be ascertained has been described elsewhere.[54]

---

44   MCA 2005, s 4(7)(b).
45   See paras. **8.37–8.39**.
46   MCA 2005, s 32(1).
47   MCA 2005, s 32(2)(a).
48   *Ibid.*
49   MCA 2005, s 32(2)(b).
50   MCA 2005, s 32(4)(b).
51   *Ibid.*
52   MCA 2005, s 32(8) and (9).
53   MCA 2005, s 32(5).
54   See, for example: Ashton *et al.* 2006, paras. 5.73–5.81; Bartlett 2005, paras. 2.123–2.134; Greaney *et al.*, 2005, Chapter 8; Jones 2005, pp.75–82.

The interested person

BEST INTERESTS

8.47 In the case of a person with incapacity, anyone interested in his or her welfare has certain limited rights when a decision has to be made as to the incapable person's 'best interests'.[55] Those rights are equivalent to the ones possessed by (a) anyone named by the incapable person in this regard and (b) anyone engaged in caring for him or her.[56]

RESEARCH

8.48 An interested person also has certain rights where it is proposed to carry out research on the person with incapacity.[57] Those rights are equivalent to the ones possessed by anyone engaged in caring for the incapable person.[58]

Comment

8.49 The MCA 2005 deputy or donee are beyond the scope of this book. The means by which they are appointed, the fact that they are accountable for the way they exercise their powers, and the great breadth of the terrain over which, at least in theory, they might range, distinguish them very clearly from a nearest relative under MHA 1983.

8.50 The functions of other statutory actors might seem rather more similar to those of the nearest relative: each, after all, has at least some expectation of being consulted about key decisions. Ultimately, however, the person named, the carer and the interested person are less significant under MCA 2005 than the nearest relative is under MHA 1983: except where research is proposed, they have no right to veto or terminate a particular intervention.

---

55   MCA 2005, s 4(7)(b).
56   See paras. **8.37–8.39** and **8.40–8.46**.
57   MCA 2005, s 32(1).
58   See paras. **8.40–8.46**.

Statutory Extracts

The Mental Health Act 1983
General provisions as to applications

11. – (3) Before or within a reasonable time after an application for the admission of a patient for assessment is made by an approved social worker, that social worker shall take such steps as are practicable to inform the person (if any) appearing to be the nearest relative of the patient that the application is to be or has been made and of the power of the nearest relative under section 23(2)(a) below.

(4) Neither an application for admission for treatment nor a guardianship application shall be made by an approved social worker if the nearest relative of the patient has notified that social worker, or the local social services authority by whom that social worker is appointed, that he objects to the application being made and, without prejudice to the foregoing provision, no such application shall be made by such a social worker except after consultation with the person (if any) appearing to be the nearest relative of the patient unless it appears to that social worker that in the circumstances such consultation is not reasonably practicable or would involve unreasonable delay.

Definition of 'relative' and 'nearest relative'

26. – (1) In this Part of this Act 'relative' means any of the following persons:-

- (a)   husband or wife;
- (b)   son or daughter;
- (c)   father or mother;
- (d)   brother or sister;
- (e)   grandparent;
- (f)   grandchild;
- (g)   uncle or aunt;
- (h)   nephew or niece.

(2) In deducing relationships for the purposes of this section, any relationship of the half-blood shall be treated as a relationship of the whole blood, and an illegitimate person shall be treated as the legitimate child of

(a) his mother, and

(b) if his father has parental responsibility for him within the meaning of section 3 of the Children Act 1989, his father.[1]

(3) In this Part of this Act, subject to the provisions of this section and to the following provisions of this Part of this Act, the 'nearest relative' means the person first described in subsection (1) above who is for the time being surviving, relatives of the whole blood being preferred to relatives of the same description of the half-blood and the elder or eldest of two or more relatives described in any paragraph of that subsection being preferred to the other or others of those relatives, regardless of sex.

(4) Subject to the provisions of this section and to the following provisions of this Part of this Act, where the patient[2] ordinarily resides with or is cared for by one or more of his relatives (or, if he is for the time being an in-patient in a hospital,[3] he last ordinarily resided with or was cared for by one or more of his relatives) his nearest relative shall be determined –

(a) by giving preference to that relative or those relatives over the other or others; and

(b) as between two or more such relatives, in accordance with subsection (3) above.

(5) Where the person who, under subsection (3) or (4) above, would be the nearest relative of a patient –

(a) in the case of a patient ordinarily resident in the United Kingdom, the Channel Islands or the Isle of Man, is not so resident; or

(b) is the husband or wife of the patient, but is permanently separated from the patient, either by agreement or under an order of a court, or has deserted or has been deserted by the patient for a period which has not come to an end; or

(c) is a person other than the husband, wife, father or mother of the patient, and is for the time being under 18 years of age

the nearest relative of the patient shall be ascertained as if that person were dead.

---

1   This provision is as amended by article 3 of the Children Act 1989 (Consequential Amendment of Enactments) Order 1991 – SI 1991 No 1881.

2   A patient is 'a person suffering or appearing to be suffering from mental disorder' – MHA 1983, s 145(1).

3   A hospital can be either (a) 'any health service hospital within the meaning of the National Health Service Act 1977' or (b) 'any accommodation provided by a local authority and used as a hospital or on behalf of the Secretary of State' under the Mental Health Act – MHA 1983, s 145(1). Alternatively, it might be (c) 'an establishment […] in respect of which a person is registered under Part II of the Care Standards Act 2000 as an independent hospital in which treatment or nursing (or both) are provided for persons liable to be detained under' the Mental Health Act – MHA 1983, s 34(1).

(6) In this section 'husband' and 'wife' include a person who is living with the patient as the patient's husband or wife, as the case may be (or, if the patient is for the time being an in-patient in a hospital, was so living until the patient was admitted), and has been or had been so living for a period of not less than six months; but a person shall not be treated by virtue of this subsection as the nearest relative of a married patient unless the husband or wife of the patient is disregarded by virtue of paragraph (b) of subsection (5) above.

(7) A person, other than a relative, with whom the patient ordinarily resides (or, if the patient is for the time being an in-patient in a hospital, last ordinarily resided before he was admitted), and with whom he has or had been ordinarily residing for a period of not less than five years, shall be treated for the purposes of this Part of this Act as if he were a relative but –

(a)   shall be treated for the purposes of subsection (3) above as if mentioned last in subsection (1) above; and

(b)   shall not be treated by virtue of this subsection as the nearest relative of a married patient unless the husband or wife of the patient is disregarded by virtue of paragraph (b) of subsection (5) above.

Children and young persons in care

27. – Where –

(a)   a patient who is a child or young person is in the care of a local authority by virtue of a care order within the meaning of the Children Act 1989; or –

(b)   the rights and powers of a parent of a patient who is a child or young person are vested in a local authority by virtue of section 16 of the Social Work (Scotland) Act 1968,

the authority shall be deemed to be the nearest relative of the patient in preference to any person except the patient's husband or wife (if any).

Nearest relative of minor under guardianship

28. – (1) Where

(a)   a guardian has been appointed for a person who has not attained the age of eighteen years; or

(b)   a residence order (as defined by section 8 of the Children Act 1989) is in force with respect to such a person,

the guardian (or guardians, where there is more than one) or the person named in the residence order shall, to the exclusion of any other person, be deemed to be his nearest relative.

(2) Subsection (5) of section 26 above shall apply in relation to a person who is, or who is one of the persons, deemed to be the nearest relative of a patient by virtue of this section as it applies in relation to a person who would be the nearest relative under subsection (3) of that section.

(3) In this section 'guardian' includes a special guardian (within the meaning of the Children Act 1989), but does not include a guardian under this Part of this Act.

(4) In this section 'court' includes a court in Scotland or Northern Ireland, and 'enactment' includes an enactment of the Parliament of Northern Ireland, a Measure of the Northern Ireland Assembly and an Order in Council under Schedule 1 of the Northern Ireland Act 1974.

Appointment by court of acting nearest relative

29. – (1) The county court may, upon application made in accordance with the provisions of this section in respect of a patient, by order direct that the functions of the nearest relative of the patient under this Part of this Act and sections 66 and 69 below shall, during the continuance in force of the order, be exercisable by the applicant, or by any other person specified in the application, being a person who, in the opinion of the court, is a proper person to act as the patient's nearest relative and is willing to do so.

(2) An order under this section may be made on the application of –

(a)   any relative of the patient;

(b)   any other person with whom the patient is residing (or, if the patient is then an in-patient in a hospital, was last residing before he was admitted); or

(c)   an approved social worker;

but in relation to an application made by such a social worker, subsection (1) above shall have effect as if for the words 'the applicant' there were substituted the words 'the local social services authority'.

(3) An application for an order under this section may be made upon any of the following grounds, that is to say –

(a)   that the patient has no nearest relative within the meaning of this Act, or that it is not reasonably practicable to ascertain whether he has such a relative, or who that relative is;

(b)   that the nearest relative of the patient is incapable of acting as such by reason of mental disorder or toher illness;

(c)   that the nearest relative of the patient unreasonably objects to the making of an application for admission for treatment or a guardianship application in respect of the patient; or

(d) that the nearest relative of the patient has exercised without due regard to the welfare of the patient or the interests of the public his power to discharge the patient from hospital or guardianship under this Part of this Act, or is likely to do so.

(4) If, immediately before the expiration of the period for which a patient is liable to be detained by virtue of an application for admission for assessment, an application under this section, which is an application made on the ground specified in subsection (3)(c) or (d) above, is pending in respect of the patient, that period shall be extended –

(a) in any case, until the application under this section has been finally disposed of; and

(b) if an order is made in pursuance of the application under this section, for a further period of seven days;

and for the purposes of this subsection an application under this section shall be deemed to have been finally disposed of at the expiration of the time allowed for appealing from the decision of the court or, if notice of appeal has been given within that time, when the appeal has been heard or withdrawn, and 'pending' shall be construed accordingly.

(5) An order made on the ground specified in subsection (3)(a) or (b) above may specify a period for which it is to continue in force unless previously discharged under section 30 below.

(6) While an order made under this section is in force, the provisions of this Part of this Act (other than this section and section 30 below) and sections 66, 69, 132(4) and 133 below shall apply in relation to the patient as if for any reference to the nearest relative of the patient there were substituted a reference to the person having the functions of that relative and (without prejudice to section 30 below) shall so apply notwithstanding that the person who was the patient's nearest relative when the order was made is no longer his nearest relative; but this subsection shall not apply to section 66 below in the case mentioned in paragraph (h) of subsection (1) of that section.

Discharge and variation of orders under s. 29

30. – (1) An order made under section 29 above in respect of a patient may be discharged by the county court upon application made –

(a) in any case, by the person having the functions of the nearest relative of the patient by virtue of the order;

(b) where the order was made on the ground specified in paragraph (a) or paragraph (b) of section 29(3) above, or where the person who was the nearest relative of the patient when the order was made has ceased to be his nearest relative, on the application of the nearest relative of the patient.

(2) An order made under section 29 above in respect of a patient may be varied by the county court, on the application of the person having the functions of the nearest relative by virtue of the order or on the application of an approved social worker, by substituting for the first-mentioned person a local social services authority or any other person who in the opinion of the court is a proper person to exercise those functions, being an authority or person who is willing to do so.

(3) If the person having the functions of the nearest relative of a patient by virtue of an order under section 29 above dies –

(a)   subsections (1) and (2) above shall apply as if for any reference to that person there were substituted a reference to any relative of the patient, and

(b)   until the order is discharged or varied under those provisions the functions of the nearest relative under this Part of this Act and sections 66 and 69 below shall not be exercisable by any person.

(4) An order under section 29 above shall, unless previously discharged under subsection (1) above, cease to have effect at the expiration of the period, if any, specified under subsection (5) of that section or, where no such period is specified –

(a)   if the patient was on the date of the order liable to be detained in pursuance of an application for admission for treatment or by virtue of an order or direction under Part III of this Act (otherwise than under section 35, 36 or 38) or was subject to guardianship under this Part of this Act or by virtue of such an order or direction, or becomes so liable or subject within the period of three months beginning with that date, when he ceases to be so liable or subject (otherwise than on being transferred in pursuance of regulations under section 19 above);

(b)   if the patient was not on the date of the order, and has not within the said period become, so liable or subject, at the expiration of that period.

(5) The discharge or variation under this section of an order made under section 29 above shall not affect the validity of anything previously done in pursuance of the order.

Special provisions as to wards of court

33. – (1) An application for the admission to hospital of a minor who is a ward of court may be made under this Part of this Act with the leave of the court; and section 11(4) above shall not apply in relation to an application so made.

(2) Where a minor who is a ward of court is liable to be detained in a hospital by virtue of an application for admission under this Part of this Act, any power exercisable under this Part of this Act or under section 66 below in relation to the patient by his nearest relative shall be exercisable by or with the leave of the court.

(3) Nothing in this Part of this Act shall be construed as authorising the making of a guardianship application in respect of a minor who is a ward of court, or the transfer into guardianship of any such minor.

(4) Where a supervision application has been made in respect of a minor who is a ward of court, the provisions of this Part of this Act relating to after-care under supervision have effect in relation to the minor subject to any order which the court may make in the exercise of its wardship jurisdiction.

Children Act 1989[4]

Parental responsibility for children

2. – (1) Where a child's father and mother were married to each other at the time of his birth, they shall each have parental responsibility for the child.

(2) Where a child's father and mother were not married to each other at the time of his birth –

(a) the mother shall have parental responsibility for the child;

(b) the father shall have parental responsibility for the child if he has acquired it (and has not ceased to have it) in accordance with the provisions of this Act.

(3) References in this Act to a child whose father and mother were, or (as the case may be) were not, married to each other at the time of his birth must be read with section 1 of the Family Law Reform Act 1987 (which extends their meaning).

(4) The rule of law that a father is the natural guardian of his legitimate child is abolished.

(5) More than one person may have parental responsibility for the same child at the same time.

(6) A person who has parental responsibility for a child at any time shall not cease to have that responsibility solely because some other person subsequently acquires parental responsibility for the child.

---

4   As amended by the Adoption and Children Act 2002, s 111(1)-(5) and s 112, and by the Civil Partnership Act 2004, s 75(1) and (2)

(7) Where more than one person has parental responsibility for a child, each of them may act alone and without the other (or others) in meeting that responsibility; but nothing in this Part shall be taken to affect the operation of any enactment which requires the consent of more than one person in a matter affecting the child.

(8) The fact that a person has parental responsibility for a child shall not entitle him to act in any way which would be incompatible with any order made with respect to the child under this Act.

(9) A person who has parental responsibility for a child may not surrender or transfer any part of that responsibility to another but may arrange for some or all of it to be met by one or more persons acting on his behalf.

(10) The person with whom any such arrangement is made may himself be a person who already has parental responsibility for the child concerned.

(11) The making of any such arrangement shall not affect any liability of the person making it which may arise from any failure to meet any part of his parental responsibility for the child concerned.

Meaning of 'parental responsibility'

3. – (1) In this Act 'parental responsibility' means all the rights, duties, powers, responsibilities and authority which by law a parent of a child has in relation to the child and his property.

(2) It also includes the rights, powers and duties which a guardian of the child's estate (appointed, before the commencement of section 5, to act generally) would have had in relation to the child and his property.

(3) The rights referred to in subsection (2) include, in particular, the right of the guardian to receive or recover in his own name, for the benefit of the child, property of whatever description and wherever situated which the child is entitled to receive or recover.

(4) The fact that a person has, or does not have, parental responsibility for a child shall not affect –

  (a)   any obligation which he may have in relation to the child (such as a statutory duty to maintain the child); or

  (b)   any rights which, in the event of the child's death, he (or any other person) may have in relation to the child's property.

(5) A person who –

  (a)   does not have parental responsibility for a particular child; but

  (b)   has care of the child,

may (subject to the provisions of this Act) do what is reasonable in all the circumstances of the case for the purpose of safeguarding or promoting the child's welfare.

Acquisition of parental responsibility by father

4. – (1) Where a child's father and mother were not married to each other at the time of his birth, the father shall acquire parental responsibility for the child if –

(a)   he becomes registered as the child's father under any of the enactments specified in subsection 1A;

(b)   he and the child's mother make an agreement (a 'parental responsibility agreement') providing for him to have parental responsibility for the child; or

(c)   the court, on his application, orders that he shall have parental responsibility for the child.

(1A) The enactments referred to in subsection (1)(a) are –

(a)   paragraphs (a), (b) and (c) of section 10(1) and of section 10A(1) of the Births and Deaths Registration Act 1953;

(b)   paragraphs (a), (b)(i) and (c) of section 18(1), and sections 18(2)(b) and 20(1)(a) of the Registration of Births, Deaths and Marriages (Scotland) Act 1965; and

(c)   sub-paragraphs (a), (b) and (c) of Article 14(3) of the Births and Deaths Registration (Northern Ireland) Order 1976.

(1B) The Secretary of State may by order amend subsection (1A) so as to add further enactments to the list in that subsection.

(2) No parental responsibility agreement shall have effect for the purposes of this Act unless –

(a)   it is made in the form prescribed by regulations made by the Lord Chancellor; and

(b)   where regulations are made by the Lord Chancellor prescribing the manner in which such agreements must be recorded, it is recorded in the prescribed manner.

(2A) A person who has acquired parental responsibility under subsection (1) shall cease to have that responsibility only if the court so orders.

(3) The court may make an order under subsection (2A) on the application –

(a)   of any person who has parental responsibility for the child; or

(b)   with the leave of the court, of the child himself,

subject, in the case of parental responsibility acquired under subsection (1)(c), to section 12(4).

(4) The court may only grant leave under subsection (3)(b) if it is satisfied that the child has sufficient understanding to make the proposed application.

Acquisition of parental responsibility by step-parent

4A. – (1) Where a child's parent ('parent A') who has parental responsibility for the child is married to, or a civil partner of, a person who is not the child's parent ('the step-parent') –

(a)   parent A or, if the other parent of the child also has parental responsibility for the child, both parents may by agreement with the step-parent provide for the step-parent to have parental responsibility for the child; or

(b)   the court may, on the application of the step-parent, order that the step-parent shall have parental responsibility for the child.

(2) An agreement under subsection (1)(a) is also 'a parental responsibility agreement', and section 4(2) applies in relation to such agreements as it applies in relation to parental responsibility agreements under section 4.

(3) A parental responsibility agreement under subsection (1)(a), or an order under subsection (1)(b), may only be brought to an end by an order of the court made on the application –

(a)   of any person who has parental responsibility for the child; or

(b)   with the leave of the court, of the child himself.

(4) The court may only grant leave under subsection (3)(b) if it is satisfied that the child has sufficient understanding to make the proposed application.

Mental Capacity Act 2005

35. Appointment of independent mental capacity advocates

(1) The appropriate authority must make such arrangements as it considers reasonable to enable persons ('independent mental capacity advocates') to be available to represent and support persons to whom acts or decisions proposed under sections 37, 39 and 39 [of MCA 2005] relate.

(2) The appropriate authority may make regulations as to the appointment of independent mental capacity advocates.

(3) The regulations may, in particular, provide -

(a) that a person may act as an independent mental capacity advocate only in such circumstances, or only subject to such conditions, as may be prescribed;

(b) for the appointment of a person as an independent mental capacity advocate to be subject to approval in accordance with the regulations.

(4) In making arrangements under subsection (1), the appropriate authority must have regard to the principle that a person to whom a proposed act or decision relates should, so far as practicable, be represented and supported by a person who is independent of any person who will be responsible for the act or decision.

(5) The arrangements may include provision for payments to be made to, or in relation to, persons carrying out functions in accordance with the arrangements.

(6) For the purpose of enabling him to carry out his functions, an independent mental capacity advocate –

(a) may interview in private the person whom he has been instructed to represent, and

(b) may, at all reasonable times, examine and take copies of –

(i) any health record,

(ii) any record of, or held by, a local authority and compiled in connection with a social services function, and

(iii) any record held by a person registered under Part 2 of the Care Standards Act 2000 (c 14)

which the person holding the record considers may be relevant to the independent mental capacity advocate's investigation.

(7) In this section, section 36 and section 37 [of MCA 2005], 'the appropriate authority' means –

(a) in relation to the provision of the services of independent mental capacity advocates in England, the Secretary of State, and

(b) in relation to the provision of the services of independent mental capacity advocates in Wales, the National Assembly for Wales.

36. Functions of independent mental capacity advocates

(1) The appropriate authority may make regulations as to the functions of independent mental capacity advocates.

(2) The regulations may, in particular, make provision requiring an advocate to take such steps as may be prescribed for the purpose of –

(a)   providing support to the person whom he has been instructed to represent ('P') so that P may participate as fully as possible in any relevant decision;

(b)   obtaining and evaluating relevant information;

(c)   ascertaining what P's wishes and feelings would be likely to be, and the beliefs and values that would be likely to influence P, if he had capacity;

(d)   ascertaining what alternative courses of action are available in relation to P;

(e)   obtaining a further medical opinion where treatment is proposed and the advocate thinks that one should be obtained.

(3) The regulations may also make provision as to circumstances in which the advocate may challenge, or provide assistance for the purpose of challenging, any relevant decision.

37. Provision of serious medical treatment by NHS body

(1) This section applies if an NHS body –

(a)   is proposing to provide, or secure the provision of, serious medical treatment for a person ('P') who lacks capacity to consent to the treatment, and

(b)   is satisfied that there is no person, other than one engaged in providing care or treatment for P in a professional capacity or for remuneration, whom it would be appropriate to consult in determining what would be in P's best interests.

(2) But this section does not apply if P's treatment is regulated by Part 4 of the Mental Health Act.

(3) Before the treatment is provided, the NHS body must instruct an independent mental capacity advocate to represent P.

(4) If the treatment needs to be provided as a matter of urgency, it may be provided even though the NHS body has not been able to comply with subsection (3).

(5) The NHS body must, in providing or securing the provision of treatment for P, take into account any information given, or submissions made, by the independent mental capacity advocate.

(6) 'Serious medical treatment' means treatment which involves providing, withholding or withdrawing treatment of a kind prescribed by regulations made by the appropriate authority.

(7) 'NHS body' has such meaning as may be prescribed by regulations made for the purposes of this section by –

(a)   the Secretary of State, in relation to bodies in England, or

(b)   the National Assembly for Wales, in relation to bodies in Wales.

38. Provision of accommodation by NHS body

(1) This section applies if an NHS body proposes to make arrangements –

(a)   for the provision of accommodation in a hospital or care home for a person ('P') who lacks capacity to agree to the arrangements, or

(b)   for a change in P's accommodation to another hospital or care home,

and is satisfied that there is no person, other than one engaged in providing care or treatment for P in a professional capacity or for remuneration, whom it would be appropriate for it to consult in determining what would be in P's best interests.

(2) But this section does not apply if P is accommodated as a result of an obligation imposed on him under the Mental Health Act.

(3) Before making the arrangements, the NHS body must instruct an independent mental capacity advocate to represent P unless it is satisfied that –

(a)   the accommodation is likely to be provided for a continuous period which is less than the applicable period, or

(b)   the arrangements need to be made as a matter of urgency.

(4) If the NHS body –

(a)   did not instruct an independent mental capacity advocate to represent P before making the arrangements because it was satisfied that subsection (3)(a) or (b) [of MCA 2005] applied, but

(b)   subsequently has reason to believe that the accommodation is likely to be provided for a continuous period –

(i)   beginning with the day on which accommodation was first provided in accordance with the arrangements, and

(ii)   ending on or after the expiry of the applicable period,

it must instruct an independent mental capacity advocate to represent P.

(5) The NHS body must, in deciding what arrangements to make for P, take into account any information given, or submissions made, by the independent mental capacity advocate.

(6) 'Care home' has the meaning given in section 3 of the Care Standards Act 2000 (c 14).

(7) 'Hospital' means –

(a)   a health service hospital as defined by section 275 of the National Health Service Act 2006 or section 206 of the National Health Act Service (Wales) Act 2006, or

(b)   an independent hospital as defined by section 2 of the Care Standards Act 2000.

(8) 'NHS body' has such meaning as may be prescribed by regulations made for the purposes of this section by –

(a)   the Secretary of State, in relation to bodies in England, or

(b)   the National Assembly for Wales, in relation to bodies in Wales.

(9) 'Applicable period' means –

(a)   in relation to accommodation in a hospital, 28 days, and

(b)   in relation to accommodation in a care home, 8 weeks.

39. Provision of accommodation by local authority

(1) This section applies if a local authority propose to make arrangements –

(a)   for the provision of residential accommodation for a person ('P') who lacks capacity to agree to the arrangements, or

(b)   for a change in P's residential accommodation,

and are satisfied that there is no person, other than one engaged in providing care or treatment for P in a professional capacity or for remuneration, whom it would be appropriate for them to consult in determining what would be in P's best interests.

(2) But this section applies only if the accommodation is to be provided in accordance with –

(a)   section 21 or 29 of the National Assistance Act 1948 (c 29), or

(b)   section 117 of the Mental Health Act,

as a result of a decision taken by the local authority under section 47 of the National Health Service and Community Care Act 1990 (c 19).

(3) This section does not apply if P is accommodated as a result of an obligation imposed on him under the Mental Health Act.

(4) Before making the arrangements, the local authority must instruct an independent mental capacity advocate to represent P unless they are satisfied that –

(a)   the accommodation is likely to be provided for a continuous period of less than 8 weeks, or

(b)   the arrangements need to be made as a matter of urgency.

(5) If the local authority –

(a)   did not instruct an independent mental capacity advocate to represent P before making the arrangements because they were satisfied that subsection (4)(a) or (b) applied, but

(b) subsequently have reason to believe that the accommodation is likely to be provided for a continuous period that will end 8 weeks or more after the day on which accommodation was first provided in accordance with the arrangements,

they must instruct an independent mental capacity advocate to represent P.

(6) The local authority must, in deciding what arrangements to make for P, take into account any information given, or submissions made, by the independent mental capacity advocate.

40. Exceptions

Sections 37(3), 38(3) and (4)[,] and 39(4) and (5) do not apply if there is –

(a) a person nominated by P (in whatever manner) as a person to be consulted in matters affecting his interests,

(b) a donee of a lasting power of attorney created by P,

(c) a deputy appointed by the court for P, or

(d) a donee of an enduring power of attorney (within the meaning of Schedule 4) created by P.

Regulations

Mental Health (Hospital, Guardianship and Consent to Treatment) Regulations 1983[1]

Performance of functions of nearest relative

14. – (1) Subject to the conditions of paragraph (2), the nearest relative of a patient may authorise in writing any person other than the patient or a person mentioned in section 26(5) (persons deemed not to be the nearest relative) to perform in respect of the patient the functions conferred upon the nearest relative by or under Part II of the Act or these regulations and may revoke such authority.

(2) The conditions mentioned in paragraph (1) are that, on making or revoking such authority, the nearest relative shall forthwith give the authority, or give notice in writing of the revocation of such authority, to –

(a)   the person authorised;

(b)   in the case of a patient liable to be detained in a hospital, the managers of that hospital;

(c)   in the case of a patient subject to guardianship, the responsible local social services authority and to the private guardian, if any.

(3) Any such authority shall take effect upon receipt of the authority by the person authorised, and any revocation of such authority shall take effect upon the receipt of the notice by the person authorised.

(4) A person for the time being authorised in accordance with the preceding paragraphs shall exercise the functions mentioned in paragraph (1) on behalf of the nearest relative.

---

1   SI 1983 No 893.

Specimen Document

Authority to perform the functions of nearest relative

I, [*insert name of nearest relative*], of [*insert full address*] am the [*state relation to patient*] of [*insert name of patient*] and his or her nearest relative within the meaning of the Mental Health Act 1983.

This authority is given pursuant to the Act, and also to Regulation 14(1) of the Mental Health (Hospital, Guardianship and Consent to Treatment) Regulations 1983.

I hereby authorise [*insert name of delegate*] to perform in respect of [*insert name of patient*] the functions conferred upon the nearest relative by the said Act.

Signed: ....

Nearest Relative

Date: ....

List of Legal Cases Cited

B (A) v B (L) (Mental Health Patient) [1980] 1 WLR 116, CA (**4.41; 4.59**)

Barnet LBC v Robin [1998] EWCA Civ 1630 (**4.65**)

Brenda Lewis v Mark Gibson [2005] EWCA Civ 587 (**4.48; 4.50**)

Brown v Stott [2001] 2 WLR 817 (**5.109**)

C v S (A Minor) (Abduction) [1990] 2 FLR 442 (**2.51**)

Dedman v British Building and Engineering Appliances Ltd [1974] 1 WLR 171 (**1.80**)

Derbyshire County Council v Maude [1999] EWCA Civ 1760 (**4.53; 4.95**)

FC v United Kingdom, Application No 37344/97, European Court of Human Rights, 7 September 1999 (**1.21**)

Fitzpatrick v Sterling Housing Association Limited [1999] 4 All ER 705 (**1.87**)

Gary Kinsey v North Mersey Community NHS Trust, Divisional Court, Sedley LJ, 21 June 1999 (**7.23**)

Harrogate BC v Simpson (1985) 17 HLR 205, CA (**1.87**)

JT v United Kingdom, Application No 26494/95, European Court of Human Rights, 30 March 2000; (2000) 1 FLR 909 (**1.21**)

M v United Kingdom, Application no 30357/03, decision of 13 February 2007 (**1.78**)

McMichael v United Kingdom (1995) 20 EHRR 205 (**5.109**)

Mohammed v Hammersmith and Fulham LBC [2002] UKHL 57 (**2.60; 2.63**)

Owen and another v Crown House Engineering Limited [1973] 3 All ER 618 (**1.80**)

R (Adrian Holloway) v Oxfordshire County Court and Oxfordshire & Buckinghamshire Mental Health Partnership NHS Trust [2007] EWHC 776 (Admin) (**4.61**)

R (C) v the London Maudsley NHS Trust and the Mental Health Review Tribunal (**1.80**)

R (E) v Bristol City Council [2005] EWHC 74 (Admin) (**1.80** *et seq*; **5.50; 5.53; 5.54; 6.13**)

R (G) v Ealing LBC [2002] EWHC Admin 1112 (**5.71**)

R (H) v Mental Health Review Tribunal, CO/2404/2000, Longmore J, 7 December 2000 (**2.2**)

R (M) v Secretary of State for Health [2003] EWHC 1094 (Admin) (**1.78**)

R (MH) v Secretary of State for Health [2005] UKHL 60 (**4.53; 4.95**)

R (SR) v Huntercombe Maidenhead Hospital [2005] EWHC 2361 (Admin) (**7.33**)

R (SSG) v Liverpool City Council and the Secretary of State for Health, CO/1220/2002, Maurice Kay
   J (**1.88; 2.27; 3.8**)

R (Stevens) v Plymouth City Council [2002] EWCA Civ 388 (**4.53; 4.59; 4.60; 5.105; 5.106;
   5.107; 5.109; 7.18; 7.19; 7.20**)

R (Tagoe-Thompson) v The Hospital Managers of the Park Royal Centre [2003] EWCA Civ 330
   (**7.30**)

R (WC) v South London and Maudsley NHS Trust and another [2001] EWHC Admin 1025 (**2.7;
   2.62; 5.61**)

R (Wirral Health Authority and Wirral Borough Council) v Dr Finnegan and DE [2001] EWHC 312
   (Admin) (**7.6**)

R v Birmingham Mental Health Trust, ex parte Phillips, CO/1501/95, Tucker J, 25 May 1995
   (**5.83**)

R v Central London County Court, ex parte London [1999] 3 All ER 991, CA (**4.64**)

R v Liverpool City Council, ex parte F, CO/2744/96, McCullough J, 16 April 1997 (**2.64; 2.70**)

R v Riverside Mental Health Trust, ex parte Huzzey (1998) 43 BMLR 167 (**7.31; 7.32**)

R v Secretary of State for Social Services, ex parte Association of Metropolitan Authorities [1986] 1 All
   ER 164 (**5.66**)

R v South Western Hospital Managers, ex parte M [1994] 1 All ER 161 (**5.33; 5.62; 5.64; 5.67;
   5.81**)

R v Uxbridge County Court, ex parte Binns [2000] MHLR 179 (**4.61**)

R v Wilson, ex parte Williamson [1996] COD 42 (**5.72**)

Re Briscoe [1998] EWHC 771 (Admin) (**5.66**)

Re D (Adoption Reports: Confidentiality) [1996] AC 593 (**4.59**)

Re D (Mental Patient: Habeas Corpus) [2000] 2 FLR 848 (**2.67; 2.68; 5.60**)

Re G K (Patient: Habeas Corpus) [1999] MHLR 128 (**7.14**)

Re GM (Patient: Consultation) [2000] MHLR 41 (**5.70**)

Re P (Adoption) (Natural Father's Rights) [1994] 1 FLR 771 (**1.80**)

Re Shearon [1996] COD 223, DC (**5.71**)

Re W (An Infant) [1971] 2 All ER 59 (**4.38; 4.39**)

Re Whitbread [1999] COD 370 (**7.24**)

Re Whitbread (Mental Patient: Habeas Corpus) [1997] EWCA Civ 1945 (**5.34; 5.63; 5.65**)

Shah v Barnet LBC [1983] 1 All ER 226, HL (**2.61**)

Smirek v Williams, Court of Appeal, 7 April 2000 (unreported) (**4.39**)

Surrey County Council Social Services Department v McMurray, Court of Appeal, 11 November 1994
   (unreported) (**4.45; 4.74**)

TP and KM v United Kingdom [2001] 2 FCR 289 (**5.109**)

W v L [1974] QB 711, CA (**4.37**)

W v United Kingdom (1977) 10 EHRR 29 (**5.109**)

References

Ashton, G., Letts, P., Oates, L. and Terrell, M. (2006) *Mental Capacity: The New Law.* London: Jordans.

Bartlett, P. (2005) *Blackstone's Guide to the Mental Capacity Act 2005.* Oxford: Oxford University Press.

Bartlett, P. and Sandland, R. (2003) *Mental Health Law: Policy and Practice* (second edition). Oxford: Oxford University Press.

Brown, R. (2006) *The Approved Social Worker's Guide to Mental Health Law.* Exeter: Learning Matters.

Clements, L. (2004) *Community Care and the Law* (third edition). London: Legal Action Group.

Department of Health (1999a) *National Service Framework for Mental Health.* London: Department of Health.

Department of Health (1999b) *Caring about Carers: National Strategy for Carers.* London: Department of Health.

Eldergill, A. (1997) *Law Relating to Mental Health Review Tribunals.* London: Sweet and Maxwell.

Greaney, N., Morris, F. and Taylor, B. (2005) *Mental Capacity Act 2005: A Guide to the New Law.* London: The Law Society.

Gostin, L. (1986) *Mental Health Services: Law and Practice.* Crayford: Shaw and Sons.

Gostin, L. and Fennell, P. (1992) *Mental Health: Tribunal Procedure* (second edition). London: Longman.

Hewitt, D. (1999) 'Mental health law.' In Christopher Baker (ed.), *The Human Rights Act 1998: A Practitioner's Guide.* London: Sweet and Maxwell.

Hewitt, D. (2001) 'The "nominated person" under a new Mental health Act.' *New Law Journal,* 10 August 2001.

Hewitt, D. (2002a) 'Do human rights impact on mental health law?' *New Law Journal,* 8 February 2002.

Hewitt, D. (2002b) 'Good in parts.' *New Law Journal,* 10 May 2002.

Hewitt, D. (2002c) 'Treatability tests.' *Solicitors Journal,* 4 October 2002.

Hewitt, D. (2003) 'Uncomfortable truths.' *New Law Journal,* 2 May 2003

Hewitt, D. (2004a) 'Between necessity and chance.' *New Law Journal,* 16 April 2004.

Hewitt, D. (2004b) 'Windmills, not giants.' *Solicitors Journal,* 5 November 2004.

Hewitt, D. (2005a) 'To improve, not bury the Draft Bill.' *New Law Journal,* 15 April 2005.

Hewitt, D. (2005b) 'Mind games.' *Solicitors Journal,* 12 August 2005, p.966.

Hewitt, D. (2006) 'Saving face?' *New Law Journal,* 14 April 2006, p.613.

Hewitt, D. (2007) 'Relative progress? *New Law Journal,* 26 January 2007, p.126.

Jones, R. (2004) *Mental Health Act Manual* (ninth edition). London: Sweet and Maxwell.

Jones, R. (2005) *Mental Capacity Act Manual.* London: Sweet and Maxwell.

Jones, R. (2006) *Mental Health Act Manual.* (tenth edition). London: Sweet and Maxwell.

Kennedy, I. and Grubb, A. (2000) *Medical Law* (third edition). London: Butterworths.

Mandelstam, M. (2005) *Community Care Practice and the Law* (third edition). London: Jessica Kingsley Publishers.

Mental Health Act Commission (1997) *Seventh Biennial Report, 1995–1997.* London: The Stationery Office.

Mental Health Act Commission (1999) *Eighth Biennial Report, 1997–1999.* London: The Stationery Office.

Mental Health Act Commission (2001) *Ninth Biennial Report, 1999–2001.* London: The Stationery Office.

Montgomery, J. (2001) *Health Care Law* (second edition). Oxford: Oxford University Press.

Porter, R. (1987) *Mind-Forg'd Manacles: A History of Madness in England – From the Restoration to the Regency.* Cambridge: Harvard University Press.

Rapaport, J. (2002) *A Relative Affair: The Nearest Relative under the Mental Health Act 1983.* Unpublished PhD thesis. Anglia Polytechnic University.

Rapaport, J. (2003) 'The ghost of the nearest relative under the Mental Health Act 1983 – past, present and future.' *Journal of Mental Health Law,* July 2003, pp.51–65.

Subject Index

Author Index